Functional Skills
English
Level 1

This CGP book is the best way to prepare for Level 1 Functional Skills English.
It covers all the major test providers, including Edexcel and City & Guilds.

Every topic is clearly explained, along with all the reading and writing skills you'll need.
There are plenty of questions to help build up your confidence, including two realistic
practice papers — with answers for everything at the back of the book.

How to access your free Online Edition

This book includes a free Online Edition to read on your PC, Mac or tablet.
You'll just need to go to **cgpbooks.co.uk/extras** and enter this code:

2607 7019 3505 2414

By the way, this code only works for one person. If somebody else has used
this book before you, they might have already claimed the Online Edition.

CGP — still the best! ☺

Our sole aim here at CGP is to produce the highest quality books —
carefully written, immaculately presented and dangerously close to being funny.

Then we work our socks off to get them out to you
— at the cheapest possible prices.

Contents

Section Two — Choosing the Right Language and Format

Section Three — Using Grammar

Section Four — Using Correct Punctuation

Section Five — Using Correct Spelling

The Writing Test

Published by CGP

Editors:
Tom Carney
Becca Lakin
Rebecca Russell
Sean Walsh

With thanks to Izzy Bowen for the proofreading.

With thanks to Jan Greenway for the copyright research.

ISBN: 978 1 78294 629 8

Printed by Elanders Ltd, Newcastle upon Tyne.
Clipart from Corel®

Photocopying more than one section of this book is not permitted, even if you have a CLA licence.
Extra copies are available from CGP with next day delivery • 0800 1712 712 • www.cgpbooks.co.uk

What is Functional Skills English?

Functional Skills are a set of qualifications

1) They're designed to give you the **skills** you need in **everyday life**.

2) There are **three** Functional Skills **subjects** — **English**, **Maths** and **ICT**.

3) You may have to sit **tests** in **one**, **two** or all **three** of these subjects.

4) Each subject has **five levels** — **Entry Level 1-3**, **Level 1** and **Level 2**.

This book is for Functional Skills English

1) There are **three** parts to Functional Skills English — **reading**, **writing** and **speaking, listening and communicating**.

2) To get a Functional Skills English qualification, you need to **pass all three parts**.

3) This book covers the **reading** and **writing** parts of **Functional Skills English Level 1**.

The papers for each exam board are slightly different — ask your teacher or tutor to make sure you know which one you're sitting.

There are two tests and a controlled assessment

1) **Speaking, listening and communicating** is tested by a **controlled assessment** in class.

2) Reading and writing are tested in **two separate tests**.

3) You might take your test on a **computer** (onscreen) or on **paper**.

Reading

- In the **test**, you have to **read** a **range of texts** and **answer questions** on them.

- Some questions might be **multiple choice** (you choose the correct answer).

- Some questions might ask you to **write** your **answer**.

- You **don't** have to write in **full sentences**.

- You **won't** lose marks if you make **spelling, punctuation** or **grammar mistakes** in your writing, but make sure your answers are **clear** and **understandable**.

Writing

- In the **test**, you will be asked to write **two texts**.

- These **two texts** will usually be **different**, for example a **letter** and an **article**.

- You **will lose marks** if your spelling, punctuation or grammar are **incorrect**.

How to Use this Book

This book summarises everything you need to know

1) This book is designed to help you **go over** what you're already learning in class.

2) Use it along with any **notes** and **resources** your teacher has given you.

3) You can work through this book from **start** to **finish**...

4) ...or you can just **target the topics** that you're **not sure** about.

Use this book to revise and test yourself

1) This book is split into **two parts** — **reading** and **writing**.

2) The topics in each part are usually **spread over two pages**:

Here's the title of the topic.

On the left-hand page there's all the important information for each topic.

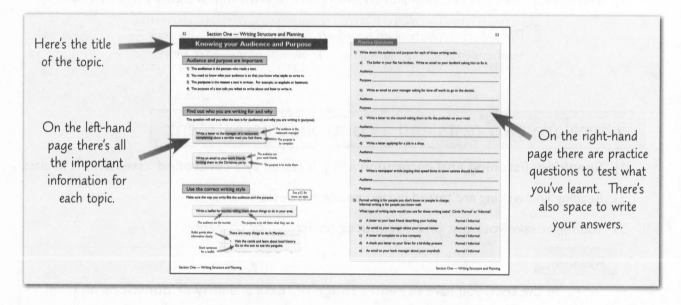

On the right-hand page there are practice questions to test what you've learnt. There's also space to write your answers.

There's lots of test-style practice

There are answers to all the practice questions and the practice papers at the end of the book.

1) There are **practice papers** at the **end** of both parts of the book.

2) These papers are based on **actual Functional Skills English assessments**.

3) This means that the questions are **similar** to the ones you'll be asked in the **real tests**.

4) They're a good way of **testing** the **skills you've learnt** under **timed conditions**.

5) This will give you a **good idea** of what to expect when you take the real test.

Using a Dictionary

You can use a dictionary in the reading paper

1) Some questions in the reading paper may advise you to use a **dictionary**.

2) You can use a dictionary to look up the **meaning** of a **tricky word** at any time in this paper.

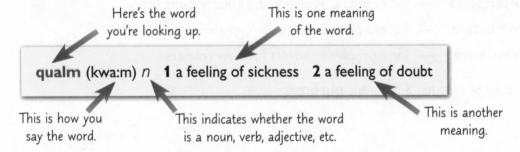

Here's the word you're looking up.

This is one meaning of the word.

qualm (kwa:m) *n* **1** a feeling of sickness **2** a feeling of doubt

This is how you say the word.

This indicates whether the word is a noun, verb, adjective, etc.

This is another meaning.

3) You **won't** be allowed to use a dictionary in the **writing paper**.

Practise using a dictionary before the test

1) The words in a **dictionary** are listed in **alphabetical order**.

2) This means all the words starting with '**a**' are **grouped together** first, then all the words starting with '**b**', and so on.

3) Each **letter** in a word is also listed in **alphabetical order**.

4) When you're looking up a word, check the words in **bold** at the **top** of **each page**.

5) These words help you work out which **page** you need to **turn to**.

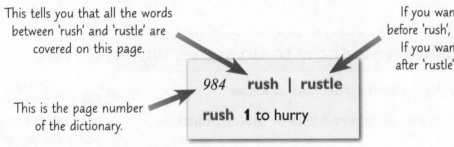

This tells you that all the words between 'rush' and 'rustle' are covered on this page.

If you want a word that comes before 'rush', turn to an earlier page. If you want a word that comes after 'rustle', turn to a later page.

984   **rush | rustle**

rush 1 to hurry

This is the page number of the dictionary.

Don't use a dictionary all the time

1) Dictionaries can be **helpful**, but **don't** use them **too often**.

2) Looking up **lots** of words will **slow you down** in the test.

3) Try looking at the **rest of the sentence** to **narrow down** what a tricky word could mean.

> If there's a word you don't recognise in this book, use a dictionary to look it up. It's a good way of practising.

The Purposes of Different Texts

Texts have different purposes

1) There are **four** main kinds of text you could come across:

- **explanatory** — for example, an article about craft workshops
- **descriptive** — for example, a review of a holiday camp
- **instructive** — for example, a recipe for cupcakes
- **persuasive** — for example, an advert for new trainers

2) Each kind of text has a different **purpose**.

Explanatory writing tells you about something

1) Explanatory texts give the reader lots of **information**.

2) They are full of **facts**. **Facts** are statements that can be proved to be **true**.

3) They often use **technical language** too.

> The Mini first went on sale in 1959. It soon became the best selling car in Europe. Over five million of them were made and many famous people, including 'The Beatles', bought them. Since 1959, the Mini has evolved. It now has an infotainment system and park assist technology.

This example contains lots of facts like dates.

'infotainment system' and 'park assist' are technical terms to do with the features of the car.

Instructive writing tells you how to do something

1) Instructive texts give the reader **instructions** to follow.

2) They are usually split up into **numbered lists** or **bullet points**.

3) They usually use **clear language** to make them easy to understand.

See p.17 for more on numbered lists and bullet points.

> - If you hear the fire alarm, stop what you are doing.
> - Make your way safely to the nearest exit.
> - Leave all of your belongings behind.

Simple language makes instructions straightforward.

Each instruction has a separate bullet point.

Read the text below, and then answer the questions underneath.

Shopping Company Creates New Jobs

It was announced yesterday that the home shopping company Goldson's Total Merchandise (GTM) is to open a new branch in Harsham. The company will open its new site on St. Peters Road in August of next year. It will employ 150 staff to run a brand new call centre and warehouse.

GTM's Managing Director, Lucy Nuttley, said, "We are delighted to have finally tied up the loose ends on this arrangement. This is an exciting development for us as a company and for the Harsham area."

Building work on the site will start immediately. GTM plans to refurbish the offices that already exist on the site, but an entirely new warehouse will be built.

GTM was founded in 2002. It quickly grew to be one of the leading home shopping companies in the UK, with offices in London, Birmingham and Newport.

1) What kind of business is Goldson's Total Merchandise? Circle your answer.

a) An internet shopping company

b) A home shopping company

c) A building company

d) An office supplies company

2) When was Goldson's Total Merchandise founded? Circle your answer.

a) 2002

b) 2013

c) 2008

d) 2004

3) Name **one** place where GTM already has offices.

....

4) a) Is this text explanatory or instructive? ....

b) How can you tell? ....

....

The Purposes of Different Texts

Persuasive writing tries to convince the reader

1) Persuasive texts might use **emotive language** to make the reader **feel** a certain way.

> The traffic situation in Little Urswell is a disgrace. Our children are put in danger every day, but the council refuse to do anything. Before long there's going to be a tragedy.

Words like 'disgrace', 'danger' and 'tragedy' make the reader feel angry so that they're more likely to agree with the writer. Mentioning 'children' makes this feeling stronger.

2) They sometimes use **facts** to persuade the reader.

> Temperatures across the world have increased by about 1°C in the last hundred years. Governments must act to fight climate change because scientists predict that temperatures will continue to rise.

Facts make writing more believable. The writer sounds like an expert.

Descriptive writing tells readers what something is like

1) It uses **describing words** like 'dusty', 'exciting' and 'silently'.

> The walk begins in a stunning location by a peaceful lake, not far from Yorley Wood. As you wander past the lake, you might see beautiful swans. The route is short but quite steep.

Describing words tell you what the walk is like.

2) Descriptive writing can also **persuade** people.

> Don't watch this terrible film. Its shallow characters aren't realistic, and their lives were so dull that I fell asleep.

These describing words try to persuade the reader not to watch the film.

Practice Questions

Read the text below, and then answer the questions underneath.

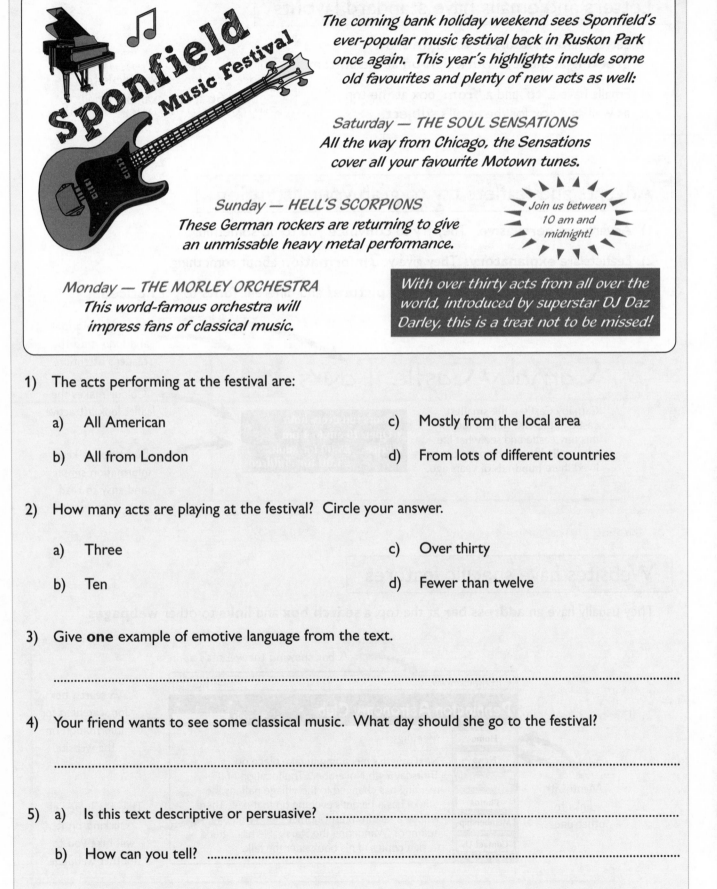

Sponfield Music Festival

The coming bank holiday weekend sees Sponfield's ever-popular music festival back in Ruskon Park once again. This year's highlights include some old favourites and plenty of new acts as well:

Saturday — THE SOUL SENSATIONS
All the way from Chicago, the Sensations cover all your favourite Motown tunes.

Sunday — HELL'S SCORPIONS
These German rockers are returning to give an unmissable heavy metal performance.

Join us between 10 am and midnight!

Monday — THE MORLEY ORCHESTRA
This world-famous orchestra will impress fans of classical music.

With over thirty acts from all over the world, introduced by superstar DJ Daz Darley, this is a treat not to be missed!

1) The acts performing at the festival are:

   a) All American

   b) All from London

   c) Mostly from the local area

   d) From lots of different countries

2) How many acts are playing at the festival? Circle your answer.

   a) Three

   b) Ten

   c) Over thirty

   d) Fewer than twelve

3) Give **one** example of emotive language from the text.

....

4) Your friend wants to see some classical music. What day should she go to the festival?

....

5) a) Is this text descriptive or persuasive? ....

   b) How can you tell? ....

....

Spotting Different Types of Text

Letters and emails have standard layouts

1) Letters have an **address**, the **date** and a **greeting** at the top, with a **sign-off** at the bottom.

2) Emails have a '**to**' and a '**from**' box at the top, as well as a box for the email's **subject**.

See p.64 for an example letter.
See p.66 for an example email.

Adverts and leaflets try to grab your attention

1) Adverts are **persuasive**. They try to **convince** you to do something.

2) Leaflets are **explanatory**. They give you **information** about something.

3) Adverts and leaflets both use **colours**, **pictures** and different **fonts** to get **noticed**.

Carnaby Castle is the **smallest** castle in the UK! Take a tour of this tiny castle and see what life was **really** like for the people who lived there **hundreds** of years ago.

- Tours run every hour
- Open 10 am to 4 pm
- Prices: £5.00 for adults
  £3.00 for children

An interesting font and logo grab the reader's attention.

Colour makes the leaflet look attractive.

Bullet points keep information simple and easy to read.

Websites have specific features

They usually have an **address bar** at the top, a **search box** and **links** to other **webpages**.

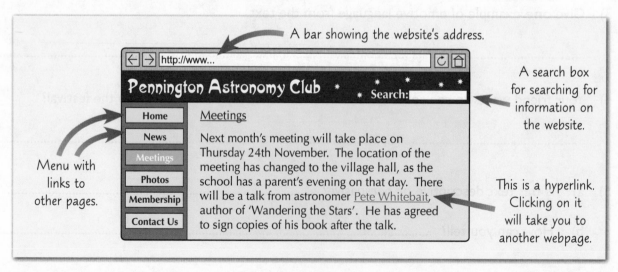

A bar showing the website's address.

Pennington Astronomy Club   Search:

Home
News
Meetings
Photos
Membership
Contact Us

Meetings

Next month's meeting will take place on Thursday 24th November. The location of the meeting has changed to the village hall, as the school has a parent's evening on that day. There will be a talk from astronomer Pete Whitebait, author of 'Wandering the Stars'. He has agreed to sign copies of his book after the talk.

A search box for searching for information on the website.

This is a hyperlink. Clicking on it will take you to another webpage.

Menu with links to other pages.

Spotting Different Types of Text

Articles are in newspapers or magazines

1) They have **headlines** to tell you what the article is **about**.

2) **Subheadings** and **columns** are used to break up the text.

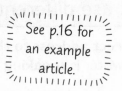
See p.16 for an example article.

Practice Questions

Look at the four text types below, and then answer the questions underneath each one.

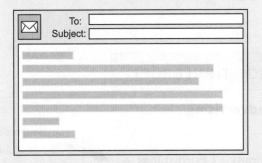

1) What type of text is this?

....

2) Name **one** feature that tells you this.

....

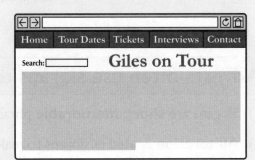

3) What type of text is this?

....

4) Name **one** feature that tells you this.

....

5) What type of text is this?

....

6) Name **one** feature that tells you this.

....

7) What type of text is this?

....

8) Name **one** feature that tells you this.

....

Spotting Language Techniques

Texts use different techniques to persuade the reader

1) A **direct address to the reader** is when it sounds as if the writer is **speaking directly** to the reader.

2) This makes the text seem more **personal**, which may help to **persuade** the reader.

> You won't believe your eyes at Catchester Animal Kingdom.

Words such as 'you' and 'your' make it seem as though the text is addressing the reader personally.

Adverts often use slogans to persuade the reader

1) Slogans are **short, memorable** phrases used in **advertising**.

2) **Alliteration** is used in slogans to make them **catchy** and easy to **remember**.

3) Alliteration is when words that are **close together** begin with the **same sound**.

> Frankie's Furnishings — fantastic furniture for less.

The repeated 'f' sound makes the slogan more memorable.

Exclamation marks can create emotion

1) **Exclamation marks** can make text seem **exciting** or **urgent**.

2) They can make the reader think that something is **important**.

3) They can also be used to emphasise **strong feelings**.

4) Exclamation marks are often used in **children's writing** because they can make texts seem more **fun** or **shocking**.

> Sale now on at The Sofa Warehouse! Don't miss these incredible offers!

The first exclamation mark makes the sale sound exciting.

The second exclamation mark highlights how incredible the writer thinks the offers are.

The 'rule of three' is used to create emphasis

1) The **'rule of three'** is when a writer uses a **list** of **three words** or **phrases** in their writing.

2) They do this to **emphasise** the point they are making.

3) This technique is often used in **persuasive writing**.

> The wedding was beautiful, heart-warming and fun.

This list of three positive adjectives emphasises the writer's positive feelings about the wedding.

Read the two texts below, and then answer the questions underneath each one.

TERRY'S TREADS
Terrific tyres you can trust.

Many people are throwing away their hard-earned money without even realising it, and you might be too. Under-inflated tyres make your car waste fuel, which means you spend more money at the petrol station. Luckily, Terry's Treads can help. We offer a free tyre check-up and reinflation from Monday to Friday. If any tyres need replacing, our prices won't be beaten! We do the hard work, so you don't have to waste your time, your petrol or your money.

1) Which **two** techniques are used in the phrase: 'Terrific tyres you can trust'?

    a)   Rule of three   c)   Direct address to the reader

    b)   Alliteration   d)   Exclamation marks

2) Write down the names of **two** other language techniques used in the text.

....

....

HYDRO WORLD

Do you need something to keep the family entertained this summer? Come to Hydro World, the country's biggest water park! With water slides, go-karting, minigolf, restaurants and more, there's something to keep everyone happy.

For a limited time, get a free child ticket with every adult ticket. What are you waiting for? Book now and kick-start the summer holiday of a lifetime!

3) Which **two** persuasive techniques are used in the text? Circle your answers.

    a)   Exclamation marks   c)   Alliteration

    b)   Direct address to the reader   d)   Rule of three

4) Give **one** example from the text of each technique you circled.

....

....

Identifying Tone and Style

Writing can have a personal or impersonal tone

1) **Personal** writing sounds like it's **talking to the reader**.

2) It's written from the writer's **point of view**, so it's full of **opinions** and it shows **emotion**.

We are all outraged by the cancellation of the bus service. It means that I will no longer be able to visit my local shops.

Personal writing gives the writer's opinions — this shows they feel angry and are critical of the cancellation.

It uses words like 'I', 'we' and 'you'.

3) **Impersonal** writing **doesn't** tell you anything about the writer's **personality**.

4) It just reports the **facts**, so it's usually **neutral** and doesn't take anybody's **side**.

Local people are outraged by the cancellation of their bus service. It means that they will no longer be able to visit their local shops.

Impersonal writing doesn't give any of its own opinions.

It uses words like 'she', 'him' and 'they'.

Writing can have a formal or informal style

1) **Formal** writing sounds **serious**. It usually has an **impersonal tone**.

2) It's used for things like **job applications** because it **sounds** more **professional**.

When wiring a plug, safety instructions must always be followed. It is better to leave it to professionals.

Formal writing doesn't use slang or shortened words. For example, it uses 'it is' instead of 'it's'.

3) **Informal** writing sounds **chatty**. It usually has a **personal tone**.

4) It's used for things like **letters** to your **family** because it's more **friendly**.

Wiring a plug is pretty dangerous. You're better off leaving it to a pro who knows what they're doing.

Informal writing uses shortened words and slang. For example, it uses the slang 'pro' instead of 'professional'.

Practice Questions

Read the text below, and then answer the questions underneath.

	From:	Electigen Power Customer Services
Reply	To:	e.l.grant@azmail.co.uk
	Subject:	RE: Power cuts at 25 Market Street

Dear Mr. Grant,

I am sorry to hear that you are unhappy with the treatment you have received from Electigen Power Services. We are proud of our customer service and we are disappointed that you feel we have not treated you well.

I would like to offer you a free month of electricity to apologise for the numerous power cuts you have suffered. This month of free electricity will begin on the 12th August and will end on the 11th September. I hope this will convince you not to change energy supplier.

Please let us know if you experience any other problems with your electricity.

Warm regards,

Reginald Sprint
Customer Services Manager

1) a) Is the tone of this email personal or impersonal? ....

    b) How can you tell?

....

....

2) Why do you think this tone has been used? Circle your answer.

    a) It sounds more professional   c) To show that Mr Grant is wrong

    b) The writer is friends with Mr Grant   d) To show that the writer cares

3) a) Is the style of this email formal or informal? ....

    b) How can you tell?

....

....

4) Why do you think this style has been used? Circle your answer.

    a) It sounds more business-like   c) To seem friendly and kind

    b) The writer is angry   d) To give information clearly

Reading Between the Lines

Facts are statements that can be proved

1) Some texts contain **facts** and **statistics**.

2) Statistics are facts based on **research**. They are usually written as **numbers** or **percentages**.

3) Phrases like '**experts say**', '**research shows**' and '**surveys show**' often introduce facts.

Cats have become the most popular pet in the UK.
Surveys show that 25% of UK households own a cat.
The number of pet cats is bound to continue increasing.

This is a fact. It can be proved.

This is a statistic. It is a percentage based on data from research.

This is not a fact. It cannot be proved.

An opinion is something the writer thinks

1) Some texts contain opinions.

2) Opinions aren't true or false. They are just **beliefs** and **can't** be proved.

3) Phrases like '**I think**', '**I believe**' or '**many people say**' show a statement is an opinion.

4) Opinions can be **presented** to look like facts. This makes them seem more **believable**.

'I think' shows this is an opinion.

I think we should only have to work four days a week.
Some people say it would make employees work harder.

This sounds like a fact, but it can't be proved. This means it's an opinion.

5) If you're **not sure** whether something is a fact or an opinion, think about whether it can be **proved**. If it **can**, it is a **fact**. If it **can't**, it is an **opinion**.

Information and ideas can be stated or implied

1) Sometimes information will be written **clearly** in the text.

Last weekend, I visited a horrible castle.

The speaker states that they visited a castle, so we know what they did. We also know that they thought the castle was 'horrible'.

2) Other times, you will need to do a bit of detective work to **find out** what the text means.

The castle was dark, dirty and freezing cold.

This description implies that the speaker didn't like the castle very much, but it isn't stated clearly.

Practice Questions

Read the text below, and then answer the questions underneath.

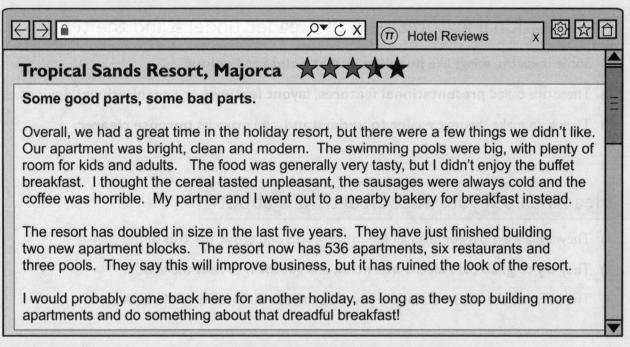

Tropical Sands Resort, Majorca ★★★★★

Some good parts, some bad parts.

Overall, we had a great time in the holiday resort, but there were a few things we didn't like. Our apartment was bright, clean and modern. The swimming pools were big, with plenty of room for kids and adults. The food was generally very tasty, but I didn't enjoy the buffet breakfast. I thought the cereal tasted unpleasant, the sausages were always cold and the coffee was horrible. My partner and I went out to a nearby bakery for breakfast instead.

The resort has doubled in size in the last five years. They have just finished building two new apartment blocks. The resort now has 536 apartments, six restaurants and three pools. They say this will improve business, but it has ruined the look of the resort.

I would probably come back here for another holiday, as long as they stop building more apartments and do something about that dreadful breakfast!

1) There are four statements from the text in the table below. Put a **tick** next to each statement to show which are facts and which are opinions.

Statement	Fact	Opinion
The food was generally very tasty		
The resort has doubled in size in the last five years		
I thought the cereal tasted unpleasant		
It has ruined the look of the resort		

2) Give another example of a negative opinion from the text that is not in the table.

....

3) Give **one** example of a statistic from the text.

....

4) a) Did the author like the apartment they stayed in? ....

b) How can you tell?

....

....

Recognising How a Text is Presented

Presentational features help the reader understand the text

1) Some texts use things like **headings**, **bullet points** and **colour**.

2) These are called **presentational features**, **layout features** or **organisational devices**.

3) They help make the text **easier to understand**, and make its **purpose clearer**.

Headlines tell you what an article is about

1) They are always **bigger** than all the other words and are at the **top** of the page.

2) They try to **grab** the reader's **attention** and get them to read the article.

3) The **tone** of the headline can give you a clue about the **mood** of the **article**.

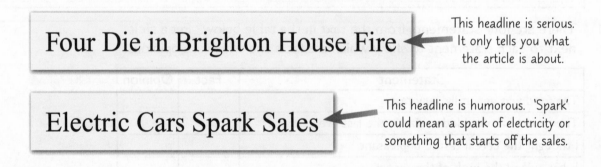

Four Die in Brighton House Fire

This headline is serious. It only tells you what the article is about.

Electric Cars Spark Sales

This headline is humorous. 'Spark' could mean a spark of electricity or something that starts off the sales.

Subheadings, columns and text boxes break up text

Newspapers and leaflets use **columns**, **subheadings** and **text boxes** to make things **clear**.

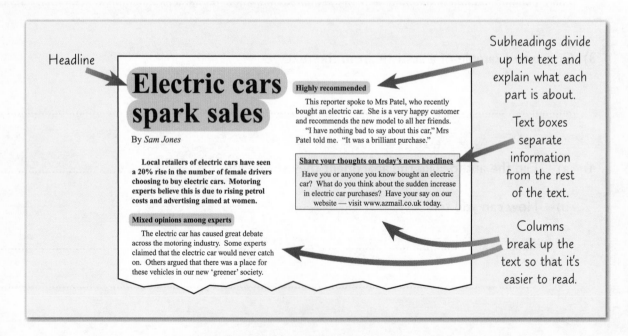

Headline

Electric cars spark sales

By *Sam Jones*

Local retailers of electric cars have seen a 20% rise in the number of female drivers choosing to buy electric cars. Motoring experts believe this is due to rising petrol costs and advertising aimed at women.

Mixed opinions among experts

The electric car has caused great debate across the motoring industry. Some experts claimed that the electric car would never catch on. Others argued that there was a place for these vehicles in our new 'greener' society.

Highly recommended

This reporter spoke to Mrs Patel, who recently bought an electric car. She is a very happy customer and recommends the new model to all her friends. "I have nothing bad to say about this car," Mrs Patel told me. "It was a brilliant purchase."

Share your thoughts on today's news headlines

Have you or anyone you know bought an electric car? What do you think about the sudden increase in electric car purchases? Have your say on our website — visit www.azmail.co.uk today.

Subheadings divide up the text and explain what each part is about.

Text boxes separate information from the rest of the text.

Columns break up the text so that it's easier to read.

Recognising How a Text is Presented

Paragraphs divide text up into chunks

1) When writers introduce a **new subject** or **idea**, they start a **new paragraph**.

2) This helps give their writing a **structure** and makes it easier to **understand**.

> Caroline, the main character, is the best thing about this book. By the end she almost feels like a friend.
>
> However, the book is let down by its plot. It is so ridiculous that it could have been thought up by a child.

A new paragraph starts here. This shows where the part about Caroline ends and the part about the plot begins.

Bullet points and numbered lists divide up texts

1) **Bullet points** separate information into **short** bits of text so it's **easier** to **read**.

2) **Numbered lists** can be used instead of bullet points.

3) This is usually for things that are **in an order**, like a set of **instructions**.

> To make a complaint, contact us by:
> * Emailing our customer service team
> * Calling our freephone helpline

Bullet points separate each piece of information. This makes the writing clear.

Sometimes parts of the text will be in a table or a footnote

1) In a **table**, use the **column headings** to help you find the information.

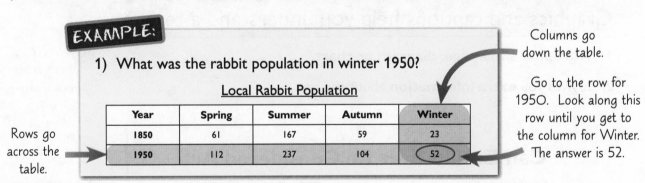

EXAMPLE:

1) What was the rabbit population in winter 1950?

Local Rabbit Population

Year	Spring	Summer	Autumn	Winter
1850	61	167	59	23
1950	112	237	104	52

Columns go down the table.

Go to the row for 1950. Look along this row until you get to the column for Winter. The answer is 52.

Rows go across the table.

2) **Footnotes** link to text at the **bottom** of the page.

3) They are usually shown by **small numbers**, but can also be shown by **symbols**, e.g. asterisks (*).

4) They make texts **easier** to understand by adding information without **interrupting** the main text.

> Every year, over 5% of the plastic we use ends up in the oceans.[1]
>
> [1] If you weighed all this plastic it would weigh about the same as three million elephants.

This means that there is extra information about this sentence.

Look for the 1 in the footnotes to find the information.

Section One — How Texts Present Ideas

Recognising How a Text is Presented

Fonts help set the tone of a text

1) A text's **font** gives you a clue about what **kind** of text it is.

2) **Serious, formal** fonts are for **serious, formal** texts.

3) **Cartoony, childish** fonts are for **light-hearted** texts or texts for **children**.

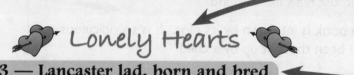

💘 Lonely Hearts 💘

Ben, 23 — Lancaster lad, born and bred.
Looking for a girl of similar age who enjoys cycling.

Amy, 32 — YOUNG~AT~HEART CLUBBER seeks man
aged 26~40 in London area to party the night away with.

The colour red is connected with love. The handwriting font makes it seem more personal.

The bold font helps divide the text up.

Capital letters can be used to emphasise key points.

Colour affects how you read a text

1) The **colour** of a **text**, or its **background**, creates an effect on the reader.

2) **Bright colours** make text look more **fun**.

3) **Dark colours** create a **serious mood** suitable for more **formal** texts.

Graphics and captions help you understand a text

1) A **graphic** is an **image**, **diagram** or **chart**.

2) It gives you **extra information** about the text.

There's more about images on p.20.

Can Graffiti Ever Be Considered Art?

Graffiti has been around for many years, and it is usually dismissed as simple vandalism. However, in recent months there has been growing pressure from the art community to recognise it as its own art form.

Graffiti on a wall in Brixton

The graphic shows the type of graffiti the text is talking about.

A caption is a bit of text that tells you more about the graphic.

Read the text below, and then answer the questions underneath.

Children's Party Games
by Jesse Gallagher

Port and Starboard

Read a command from the list on the right (or any command of your own), and tell the children to do the appropriate action. After a while, start removing the last child to do the action, until only one is left. This child is the winner.

Pass the Parcel

Wrap a present in about 10 layers of wrapping paper.[1] Play some music. Everyone sits in a circle and passes the parcel from one person to the next. When the music stops, the person holding the parcel removes ONE layer of wrapping. Repeat until the last layer has been removed. The winner keeps the present.

[1] You could try putting sweets or dares between each layer of the wrapping paper.

Commands

• **Port** (Run to the left side of the room)
• **Starboard** (Run to the right side)
• **Submarines** (Lie on the floor)
• **Climb the rigging** (Run on the spot)
• **Mess deck** (Sit on the floor)
• **Up periscope** (Hands in the air)

1) The **main** purpose of this text is to:

a) Tell children how to have fun

b) Teach the rules of 'Port and Starboard'

c) Describe how to throw a kid's party

d) Give ideas for party games to play

2) Give **one** presentational feature that shows that the article is light-hearted.

....

3) List **two** ways the article has been presented and say how they help the reader to understand the article better.

a) Presentational feature: ....

This helps the reader's understanding because: ....

....

b) Presentational feature: ....

This helps the reader's understanding because: ....

....

Working Out Meaning from Images

Images can give you extra information

1) You might have to use an image to find information that **isn't written** in the text itself.

2) Start by **quickly looking** at the image for any **obvious** things that can give you more information.

3) Think about what the image shows — are there any objects, people, animals or something else?

4) Think about **where** was the image taken.

The image shows a group of seven people.

They are in an office.

Look at images carefully

1) After a quick scan, look more closely at the image to find **less obvious** details.

2) If an image shows people, what are they **doing**? Do they look happy or sad?

3) If an image shows a landscape or an object, what **other details** can you see around it?

They look happy.

The office is bright and modern.

They are all young adults.

Some of them are holding drinks.

They are watching a presentation.

Think about what you can see

1) Use any extra information you learn from images to help you **understand** the text **better**.

2) **Clues** from an image can help you work out information that **isn't obviously stated**.

It is a fun place to work.

The dress code is not formal.

Job Vacancy — Sales Executive

We're looking for determined, hard-working people to join our growing sales team (pictured). No previous experience necessary, but you must be confident and friendly.

The job involves working in groups.

The job involves charts and graphs.

The company hires a lot of young people.

Look at the text below, and then answer the questions underneath.

Paid Apprenticeships Available

1. If you're ambitious, good with your hands and have a keen interest in engineering, then we want you.

2. Our well-paid apprenticeships offer some of the best training in the business. With our dedicated and experienced trainers, you'll quickly develop the skills you need to excel.

3. In just three years, you could be a fully qualified Motor Vehicle Service and Maintenance Technician. By the end of your training, you'll be an expert in vehicle security systems, engines, exhausts and car electronics.

4. You can download an application form and more information online. Submit your completed form and a copy of your CV on the jobs section of our website.

1) Which option below best describes what the image above is trying to show? Circle your answer.

a) A garage

b) An engineer teaching an apprentice

c) A group meeting

d) A car

2) Circle **two** other details that you can see in the **image**.

a) There are two people working on another car

b) The apprenticeship is hard work

c) The application process is easy

d) It is a bright working environment

3) Match the images below to paragraphs 2, 3 and 4 above. You must only use each number once.

a)

....

b)

....

c)

....

4) Circle **two** pieces of information that you can **only** work out from the **image**.

a) You wear protective clothing

b) It's only part-time

c) It's well-paid

d) You get one-on-one training

Section One — How Texts Present Ideas

Comparing Different Texts

Texts can have similarities and differences

1) You may be asked to **compare** two different texts.

2) You might need to compare:

   • the **information** they give to the reader

   • the **ideas** and **opinions** they express.

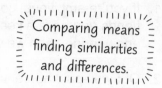

Comparing means finding similarities and differences.

EXAMPLE:

1) Compare Text A and Text B.
   a) Give **two** opinions that are the same in Text A **and** Text B.
   b) Give **three** different benefits, **one** from Text A and **two** from Text B.

You should only look for opinions that are the same in Text A and Text B.

You should only look for benefits that are different in Text A and Text B.

Think about the main points in both texts

1) To find similarities and differences, read each text **carefully**.

2) Think about what the main **points** and **opinions** are in each text.

3) Compare the points and opinions in each text to see how they are **similar** and **different**.

Remi Valentine's **new album breaks sales records**

Her song 'Trust Me' has shot to the top of the charts. People are calling it the **best song** of the last few years.

On the other hand, the final song on the album, 'Wonder', has not been quite so successful. Unlike the other songs on the album, it is the only one that has left fans **disappointed**.

Both texts are about the new album.

Both texts mention that the album is record-breaking.

The texts give similar opinions on the song 'Trust Me'.

The texts give different opinions on the song 'Wonder'.

Andre

Have you heard Remi Valentine's **new album**?

It's incredible. She's already broken all kinds of **sales records**.

The song called 'Trust Me' is really sad, but **really good**.

You should listen to 'Wonder' first. It's the **best song** by far.

Practice Questions

Read the two texts below, and then answer the questions underneath.

Text A

Hazelcroft Nursery
Birch Street, Bronton

Hazelcroft Nursery offers the best childcare in the Bronton area. We provide care for children between six months and four years old, and we're open every day between 8:00am and 6:00pm.

We have two spacious, warm buildings with plenty of room for games, arts and crafts. There is also a large garden at the rear of the building which gives children plenty of room to play outside on sunny days.

Our fully trained staff play educational games with the children every day to help support early reading and writing skills. Your children will never be bored at Hazelcroft. Call today to learn more!

Text B

Looking for childcare near Bronton

Oliver
Hi guys, I'm going back to work soon and I'm looking for a nursery for my daughter. Do you have any suggestions?

Amina
My two children go to Hazelcroft Nursery. It's the best nursery in the area, and they're even open on weekends. My son loves it because he gets to draw and paint every day.

Eric
Sorry, I disagree about Hazelcroft. My daughter found it really boring. I thought the garden was really small, and the buildings were dingy and cold.

Amina
Really? I've never thought that. I've always been really impressed. The people who work there are friendly and they've had lots of training. Plus, they help my daughter with her reading and writing.

1) Put a **tick** next to each statement to show whether the information can be found in **Text A**, **Text B** or **both**.

Statement	Text A	Text B	Both
The nursery is open from 8:00am – 6:00pm			
The nursery buildings are warm			
The nursery buildings are cold			
The nursery is open on weekends			

2) Give **one more** idea that is the **same** in Text A and Text B.

....

3) Text A and Text B both include **opinions** about the **garden** at Hazelcroft Nursery.

   a) Are these opinions similar or different? ....

   b) How can you tell?

   ....

   ....

Picking Out the Main Points

Skim the text to work out the main points

1) You **don't** need to read **all** of a text to find the **main points**.

2) Move your eyes **quickly** over the text, looking for **key words**.

3) **Key words** are the **most important words** in a piece of text.

4) They are words that tell you **who, what, where, when, why** and **how**.

5) **Underline** any key words in a text and use them to find the information you need.

> Key words might be specialist words (see p.26).

> Not much is known about the <u>origins of Stonehenge</u>. <u>Nobody knows when</u> it was built, but most historians think it must have been between <u>3000 and 2000 BC</u>.

The main points from the text are underlined. They tell you what the text is about.

> <u>Staying inside</u> watching television every day is <u>dull</u> and <u>unhealthy</u>. There are many <u>exciting</u> and <u>healthy</u> <u>outdoor activities</u> that are available in the area, like jogging, sports teams and rowing. <u>Get involved</u>!

The key words tell you that this text is trying to persuade people to do outdoor activities.

The most important point usually comes first

1) Each **paragraph** in a text has its **own main point**.

2) The **most important point** is usually in the **first paragraph**.

> This newly decorated detached house is in a fantastic area on the outskirts of Sanditon. Its location is quiet and rural, but still within easy reach of the town centre.
>
> The property has four bedrooms, a lounge, a fitted kitchen, a dining room and two bathrooms.

The location of the house is the most important point. It's in the first paragraph.

The second paragraph gives extra details.

Practice Questions

Read the text below, and then answer the questions underneath.

Search: [ ]

| Home | Shops | Cakes | Recipes | Awards | FAQs | Contact |

Annette Grey
Managing Director

Frequently Asked Questions

How did you get into baking? I've loved baking since I was a child. One of my earliest memories is of adding flour to a cake mixture with the bowl balanced on a stool. I was in my grandmother's kitchen and it went absolutely everywhere! I must have been about five.

How did you turn your hobby into a business? I left school at 17, when I got pregnant, and I didn't really know what to do. I started baking cakes for my daughter's birthday parties. Soon the other mothers were paying me to bake for their kids too. I guess it was an accident, really.

What would you do if you weren't a baker? I always wanted to be in the fire service. I really admire the incredible courage of firefighters.

1) Name **one** presentational feature that tells you this is a website.

....

2) What is the **main** point of this text? Circle your answer.

    a) To describe Annette's bakery   c) To tell the reader about Annette's life

    b) To tell people how to start a business   d) To convince people to become firefighters

3) How did Annette get into baking? Circle your answer.

    a) She couldn't be a firefighter   c) She hated school

    b) Her grandmother ran a bakery   d) She baked cakes for children's birthdays

4) How old was Annette when she left school?

....

5) Why has Annette always wanted to be in the fire service?

....

Understanding Specialist Words

Some texts use words that are specific to a topic

1) Some words are associated with particular **topics** — these are known as **specialist** words.

2) For example, the words '**runway**' and '**departures**' are specialist words for the topic of **airports**.

3) Specialist words are **usually** (but not always) used to talk about the topics they're linked to.

> If you want to visit someone who is in hospital, make sure you know which ward they are staying in. The nurse who is on duty will show you to the patient. Most wards have visiting times, so check these before you set off.

The specialist words in this text are to do with hospitals.

4) Specialist words can have a **specific meaning** within each topic they're associated with.

5) For example, 'runway' has a different meaning when linked with **airports** than with **fashion**.

Work out what unfamiliar words mean by looking around them

If you're **not sure** what a word means, reading the **rest of the text** might give you a **clue**.

The rest of the text tells you that students will learn to cook and serve food, so you can make a good guess that 'catering' means 'cooking and serving food'.

> **New course at Sunnyside College**
>
> Next year, Sunnyside College will offer a new catering course. Students will learn how to cook and serve a range of dishes. Students can also do work experience in a restaurant.

Look up new words in a dictionary

See p.3 for more on using a dictionary.

1) You can also use a **dictionary** to look up the **meaning** of specialist words.

2) Look out for any specialist words in your **daily life** or while you are **revising**.

3) Use a dictionary to **look them up** and find out what they mean.

4) Making this a **habit** will help you spot specialist words more easily in the reading test.

5) It could also **save** you **time** in the test, as using a dictionary too often may **slow you down**.

Practice Questions

Read the text below, and then answer the questions underneath.

JOB VACANCY — PHARMACY ASSISTANT

The staff at Meadowhill Lane Pharmacy are looking to hire a Pharmacy Assistant on a temporary contract to cover an employee on maternity leave. Experience is desirable but not compulsory as the successful candidate will receive appropriate training.

Responsibilities and Duties

• Supply prescription medication under the supervision of a senior pharmacist.

• Liaise with surgeries to gather correct and up-to-date patient information.

• Administrative tasks such as restocking inventory and answering the phone.

Skills Required

• Discretion is important as you will be dealing with confidential patient information.

• You will have some mathematical and scientific skills.

---

1) Why are Meadowhill Lane Pharmacy hiring a new Pharmacy Assistant? Circle your answer.

   a) Their pharmacy is getting busier

   b) They fired their last assistant

   c) The current assistant was promoted

   d) To cover maternity leave

2) For each specialist word below, suggest a replacement word or phrase with the same meaning. Use a dictionary to help you.

   a) compulsory ....

   b) confidential ....

3) Give one clue from the text that shows that 'Discretion' means 'careful behaviour'.

   ....

   ....

4) Define the following specialist words by using the text above. If you get stuck, look the word up in a dictionary.

   a) liaise ....

   b) administrative ....

   c) inventory ....

Using Layout to Help

The layout of a text can help you find details

1) **Layout features**, like subheadings and footnotes, tell you **where** different information is.

2) Use them to decide which **part** of a text to **check first**.

3) Then **scan** this part of the text to find the **details** you're looking for.

There's more on layout features on p.16-18.

Bold text highlights the key words in each section.

Watch out for footnotes with extra information.

Subheadings show you where to find each bit of information.

To read a table, find the correct row and move your finger along until you find the information you're looking for.

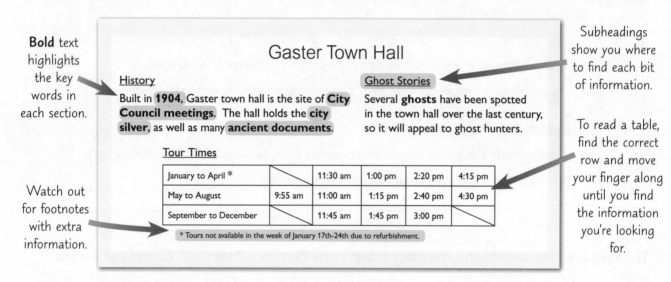

Gaster Town Hall

History
Built in **1904**, Gaster town hall is the site of **City Council meetings**. The hall holds the **city silver**, as well as many **ancient documents**.

Ghost Stories
Several **ghosts** have been spotted in the town hall over the last century, so it will appeal to ghost hunters.

Tour Times

January to April *		11:30 am	1:00 pm	2:20 pm	4:15 pm
May to August	9:55 am	11:00 am	1:15 pm	2:40 pm	4:30 pm
September to December		11:45 am	1:45 pm	3:00 pm	

* Tours not available in the week of January 17th-24th due to refurbishment.

Use subheadings to find out what a section is about

1) **Subheadings** divide text up into **sections** about **different topics**.

2) Use them to narrow down your search for **specific information** in a text.

3) Subheadings are usually in a **bigger font**, **underlined** or **bold**.

This subheading tells you this section is about the times of year to visit Hereford.

This subheading tells you this section is about places you can stay in Hereford.

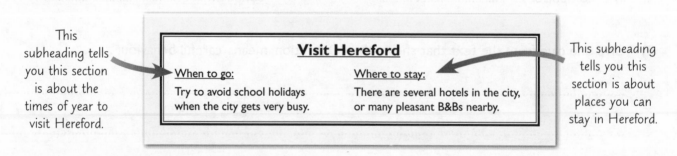

Visit Hereford

When to go:
Try to avoid school holidays when the city gets very busy.

Where to stay:
There are several hotels in the city, or many pleasant B&Bs nearby.

Use paragraphs to find more detail

1) If there's more than one paragraph under a subheading, read the **start** of each paragraph to learn what each one is about.

2) When you find the paragraph that has the information you need, **read it in full**.

3) If you have time, read the **other paragraphs** to make sure you haven't **missed** anything.

Practice Questions

Read the text below, and then answer the questions underneath.

Weather Forecast — Monday

Scotland & Northern England
Warm, dry and sunny conditions for the whole day.

Wales & South West England
Low clouds, with showers likely later in the day.

Northern Ireland
Low clouds with outbreaks of drizzly rain. Coastal areas may experience mist and fog patches.

Southern England & Midlands
Overcast with sunny intervals throughout the morning. Clouds will clear later in the day.

Tomorrow's weather
Sunny intervals over most of the country, with warm showers likely in western areas. Strong winds in the south west and north. Eastern areas will be sunny and dry for most of the day.

Longer-term forecast
The weather for the rest of the week is likely to remain changeable, before brightening up at the weekend. Expect pleasant sunshine and cool breezes on both Saturday and Sunday.

Looking further ahead towards the summer, this year is predicted to be hot and dry. A repeat of last August's record-breaking temperatures is likely, with low levels of rainfall expected.

1) What will the weather be like in Southern England & Midlands on Monday? Circle your answer.

a) Warm, dry and sunny

b) Low clouds with outbreaks of drizzly rain

c) Overcast with sunny intervals

d) Stormy

2) What areas of Northern Ireland might see patches of fog on Monday?

....

3) What is the subheading of the section that tells you about the weather on Tuesday?

....

4) How will the weather change by the end of the week? Circle your answer.

a) It will become sunnier

b) It will become stormier

c) There will be more wind and rain

d) There will be a drought

5) Write down the **first three** words of the paragraph that tells you about weather in summer.

....

Using Layout to Help

A website's menu tells you what is on each webpage

1) Some websites have a **menu** that tells you what the pages of the website **are about**.

2) The menu will often be a **list** of **links** that lead to different webpages.

The menu on this website includes links to different pages of the website.

The webpage you're currently on will often be made clear in the menu — the different colour here tells you that you are on the 'Home' page.

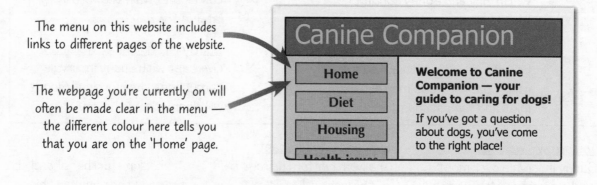

Canine Companion

| Home |
| Diet |
| Housing |
| Health issues |

Welcome to Canine Companion — your guide to caring for dogs!

If you've got a question about dogs, you've come to the right place!

3) Sometimes websites use **tabs** instead of a menu.

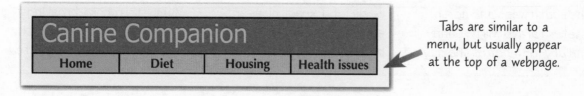

Canine Companion

| Home | Diet | Housing | Health issues |

Tabs are similar to a menu, but usually appear at the top of a webpage.

An index is a list of key topics

1) An **index** lists a text's **main topics** in **alphabetical order**.

2) It's usually found at the **end** of a text.

3) You can use an index to find out which **pages** have information about the topic you're looking for.

Turn to p.115 of this book to see its index.

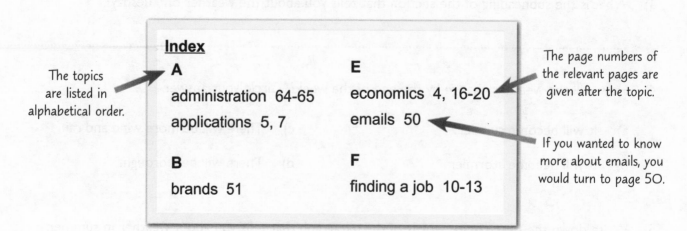

The topics are listed in alphabetical order.

Index

A

administration 64-65

applications 5, 7

B

brands 51

E

economics 4, 16-20

emails 50

F

finding a job 10-13

The page numbers of the relevant pages are given after the topic.

If you wanted to know more about emails, you would turn to page 50.

Read the text below, and then answer the questions underneath.

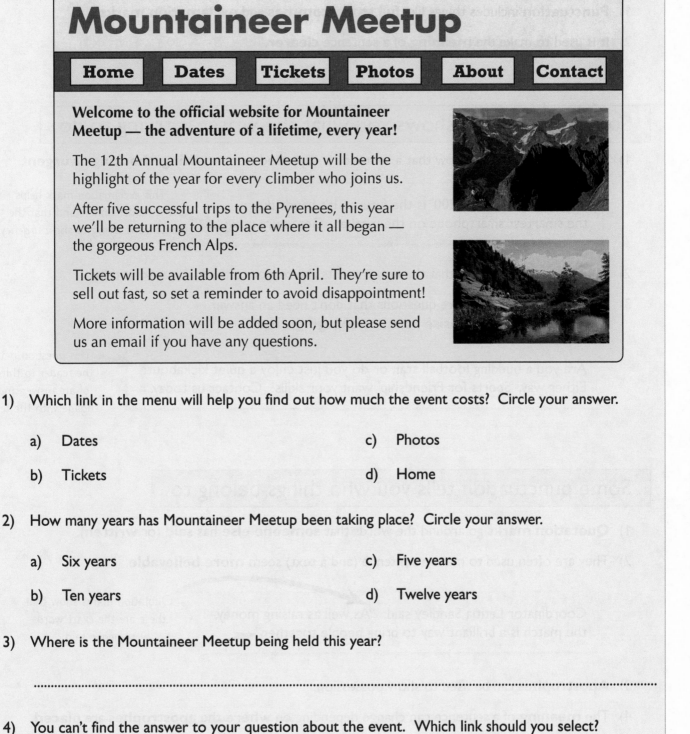

1) Which link in the menu will help you find out how much the event costs? Circle your answer.

    a) Dates   c) Photos

    b) Tickets   d) Home

2) How many years has Mountaineer Meetup been taking place? Circle your answer.

    a) Six years   c) Five years

    b) Ten years   d) Twelve years

3) Where is the Mountaineer Meetup being held this year?

    ....

4) You can't find the answer to your question about the event. Which link should you select?

    ....

5) Which of the following words is a key word? Circle your answer.

    a) year   b) gorgeous   c) Pyrenees   d) please

Using Punctuation to Help

Punctuation affects the meaning of a sentence

1) **Punctuation** includes things like **full stops**, **commas** and **exclamation marks**.

2) It is used to make the **meaning** of a sentence **clearer**.

Some punctuation shows you what the writer is trying to do

1) **Exclamation marks** show that a sentence is supposed to be **exciting**, **shocking** or **urgent**.

> The new 'Defiance Z200' is the future. It's hands down the smartest smartphone on the market. Get yours now!

This exclamation mark helps the reader understand that the sentence is trying to show urgency.

2) **Question marks** show that the writer wants the reader to think about something.

3) **Rhetorical questions** are questions that don't need an answer.
They are used to **emphasise** points or **engage** the reader.

> Are you a budding football star, or do you just enjoy a quiet kickabout? Either way, 'Sports for Friendship' want your skills! Contact us today.

This question gets the reader to think of an answer and engage with the text.

Some punctuation tells you who things belong to

1) **Quotation marks** go around the words that **someone else** has **said** (or **written**).

2) They are often used to make a sentence (and a text) seem **more believable**.

> Coordinator Letitia Sandley said: "As well as raising money, the match is a brilliant way to bring people together."

Quotation marks show that these are the exact words someone said.

3) **Apostrophes** can be used to show possession.

4) The **meaning** of a sentence can change depending on **where** the **apostrophes** are **placed**.

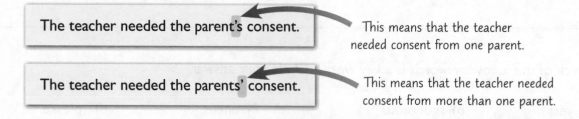

> The teacher needed the parent's consent.

This means that the teacher needed consent from one parent.

> The teacher needed the parents' consent.

This means that the teacher needed consent from more than one parent.

Practice Questions

Read the text below, and then answer the questions underneath.

TOWN CELEBRITY TO AWARD TROPHY TO WINNING SCHOOL
by Rosie Chaplin

Nights are shorter, days are warmer, flowers are in full bloom and everyone wants to be outside. These are all the classic signs that tell us summer has finally arrived. And of course, the arrival of summer also means the start of the hotly anticipated County Youth Athletics Championship (CYAC).

This year, scores of athletes from our county's secondary schools will compete not just for medals, but for the attention of former pupil turned professional hurdler, Susan Chao.

Chao won Wyreside College many medals when she competed in CYAC events herself.

Chao, renowned for winning gold in the 400 m hurdles at the 2018 National Athletics Tournament, was asked by the mayor to award the coveted CYAC trophy to the school with the most medals at the end of the week.

"This community has known Susan since she was a schoolgirl. She has been an inspiration to so many children in our local area. We're thrilled that she has agreed to this!" said Mayor Hamilton.

In a later interview, Chao said: "How could I say no? I wouldn't be where I am today without the school's support and the encouragement of the local people. It's an honour to have been asked."

Dates are still being finalised, but the first CYAC event is currently expected to take place on Monday 2nd July, with the final events and award ceremony taking place on Friday 6th July.

1) Why does Susan Chao use a rhetorical question? Circle your answer.

   a)   To end what she is saying

   b)   She needs answers

   c)   To emphasise what she is saying

   d)   To make what she's saying clearer

2) How is Mayor Hamilton feeling? Circle your answer.

   a)   excited   b)   confused   c)   angry   d)   amused

3) What type of punctuation shows how Mayor Hamilton feels?

....

4) What does the apostrophe in the phrase "the school's support" tell you? Circle your answer.

   a)   The support came from different schools

   b)   The school teaches support skills

   c)   The school was not supportive

   d)   The support came from one school

Answering Tricky Questions

Some questions ask you to understand information

Harder questions might ask you to **use** facts, not just **find** them.

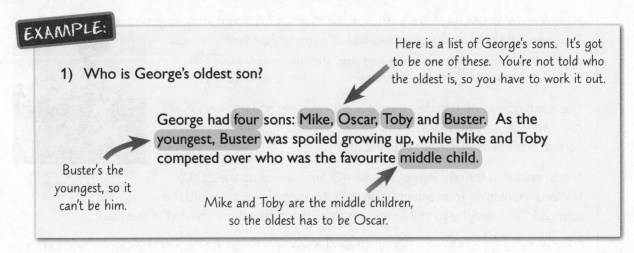

EXAMPLE:

1) Who is George's oldest son?

Here is a list of George's sons. It's got to be one of these. You're not told who the oldest is, so you have to work it out.

George had four sons: Mike, Oscar, Toby and Buster. As the youngest, Buster was spoiled growing up, while Mike and Toby competed over who was the favourite middle child.

Buster's the youngest, so it can't be him.

Mike and Toby are the middle children, so the oldest has to be Oscar.

The answer might be unclear for multiple-choice questions

1) In multiple-choice questions you'll be given a **right** answer and some **wrong** ones.

2) Some **wrong** answers might **sound right**.

3) **Rule out** the **options** that are **definitely wrong** until you're left with the **right answer**.

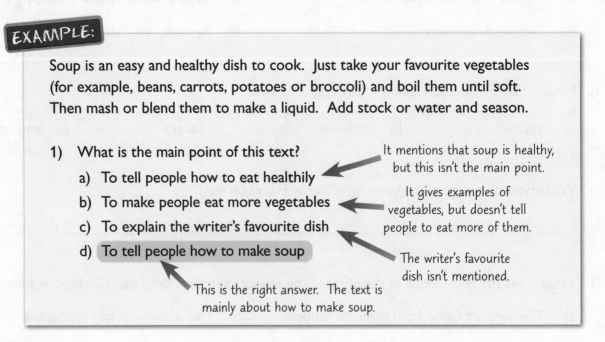

EXAMPLE:

Soup is an easy and healthy dish to cook. Just take your favourite vegetables (for example, beans, carrots, potatoes or broccoli) and boil them until soft. Then mash or blend them to make a liquid. Add stock or water and season.

1) What is the main point of this text?

a) To tell people how to eat healthily

b) To make people eat more vegetables

c) To explain the writer's favourite dish

d) To tell people how to make soup

It mentions that soup is healthy, but this isn't the main point.

It gives examples of vegetables, but doesn't tell people to eat more of them.

The writer's favourite dish isn't mentioned.

This is the right answer. The text is mainly about how to make soup.

Practice Questions

Read the text below, and then answer the questions underneath.

The Stanleybridge Observer Online

Travelling Hero Returns

Joseph Redman has been racing in his wheelchair for the last five years, but his latest challenge was a bit different. Instead of competing in a race against other wheelchair users, he has wheeled himself from Land's End to John O'Groats. So far he has raised more than £5000 for charity.

Redman set off on Tuesday 1st October, after a year of tough training. He arrived at his first checkpoint five days later, suffering from a cold. This slowed him down for the rest of his challenge, and he finally finished on Thursday 24th after eighteen more days — six days later than he'd planned.

Support Joseph!
Click here to donate.

After a rest, Joseph said he was thrilled with his performance.

"Climbing the hills was tough, but going downhill I could just let myself roll all the way. You can't do that if you're running!"

If you'd like to watch Joseph's video diary, visit our home page. If you'd like to contribute to Joseph's chosen charities, please click on the button to the left and follow the instructions.

1) What day of the week did Joseph arrive at his first checkpoint? Circle your answer.

a) Friday   c) Saturday

b) Sunday   d) Tuesday

2) What is the **main** point of this article? Circle your answer.

a) To tell people about Joseph's challenge   c) To advertise Joseph's charity

b) To persuade people to visit Land's End   d) To tell people about wheelchairs

3) How many days late did Joseph arrive at his destination? Circle your answer.

a) 18   c) 6

b) 5   d) 24

4) What should you do if you want to watch a video about his challenge? Circle your answer.

a) Click on the red button   c) Go to the website's home page

b) Look out for it on the news   d) Donate to Joseph's cause

Answering Tricky Questions

Some questions ask about a text's purpose

You have to read **all** of a text carefully to work out its **purpose**.

EXAMPLE:

The car was travelling quickly along the road when a cyclist rode out from a driveway a few metres in front of it. He had a bright red bike and was wearing reflective clothes, with a green helmet. The car had to swerve off the road to avoid the cyclist. It hit a tree and was damaged. The cyclist rode off.

1) What is the purpose of this text?

   a) To persuade the police to arrest the cyclist
   b) To complain about the speed limit
   c) To describe a road accident
   d) To persuade cyclists to wear helmets

It doesn't give any opinions about whether the cyclist should be arrested.

It doesn't say that the speed limit is too fast or too slow.

It gives a description of what made the car crash into the tree. This is the right answer.

It only mentions the green helmet the cyclist was wearing.

Pick information carefully when you write your own answer

1) **Read** each question **carefully** and work out what information **fits** best.

2) You might have to **ignore** a lot of information.

3) Look at the **number of marks**. **Write one thing** for each mark.

For the reading test, you don't have to write in full sentences.

EXAMPLE:

1) What does the report suggest that the council should do?

The recent accident on Greenley Road was caused by a driver going too fast along the road. The cyclist's driveway is hidden from the road, so the driver did not know to slow down. The cyclist should have looked before exiting.

To prevent another accident like this, the council should build speed bumps along this road. The owner of the driveway should also put up a mirror so he can see the road when he pulls out of his drive.

The first paragraph is about what caused the accident. You can ignore it.

This sentence tells you what the council should do. This is the answer.

The last sentence is about what the driveway's owner should do, so you can ignore it as well.

Practice Questions

Read the text below, and then answer the questions underneath.

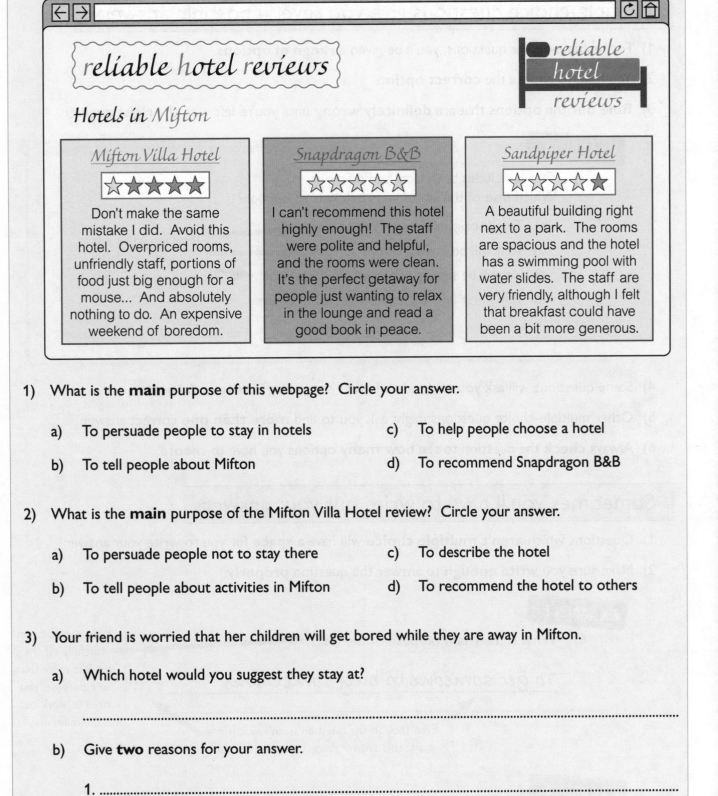

reliable hotel reviews

Hotels in Mifton

Mifton Villa Hotel

★★★★★

Don't make the same mistake I did. Avoid this hotel. Overpriced rooms, unfriendly staff, portions of food just big enough for a mouse... And absolutely nothing to do. An expensive weekend of boredom.

Snapdragon B&B

★★★★★

I can't recommend this hotel highly enough! The staff were polite and helpful, and the rooms were clean. It's the perfect getaway for people just wanting to relax in the lounge and read a good book in peace.

Sandpiper Hotel

★★★★★

A beautiful building right next to a park. The rooms are spacious and the hotel has a swimming pool with water slides. The staff are very friendly, although I felt that breakfast could have been a bit more generous.

1) What is the **main** purpose of this webpage? Circle your answer.

   a)   To persuade people to stay in hotels   c)   To help people choose a hotel

   b)   To tell people about Mifton   d)   To recommend Snapdragon B&B

2) What is the **main** purpose of the Mifton Villa Hotel review? Circle your answer.

   a)   To persuade people not to stay there   c)   To describe the hotel

   b)   To tell people about activities in Mifton   d)   To recommend the hotel to others

3) Your friend is worried that her children will get bored while they are away in Mifton.

   a)   Which hotel would you suggest they stay at?

      ....

   b)   Give **two** reasons for your answer.

      1. ....

      ....

      2. ....

      ....

Different Types of Question

Multiple-choice questions give you several possible answers

1) For multiple-choice questions, you'll be given a **range of options**.

2) You have to choose the **correct option**.

3) **Rule out** the **options** that are **definitely wrong** until you're left with the **right answer**.

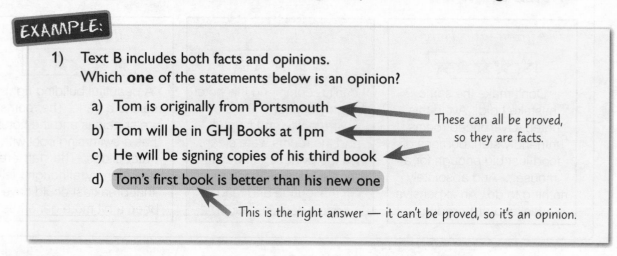

EXAMPLE:

1) Text B includes both facts and opinions.
   Which **one** of the statements below is an opinion?

   a) Tom is originally from Portsmouth
   b) Tom will be in GHJ Books at 1pm
   c) He will be signing copies of his third book
   d) Tom's first book is better than his new one

These can all be proved, so they are facts.

This is the right answer — it can't be proved, so it's an opinion.

4) Some questions will ask you to decide whether something is **true** or **false**.

5) Other multiple-choice questions might ask you to find **more than one** correct answer.

6) Always **check** the question to see **how many** options you have to choose.

Sometimes you'll have to write out your answer

1) Questions which **aren't multiple choice** will have a **space** for you to write your answer.

2) Make sure you **write enough** to answer the question **properly**.

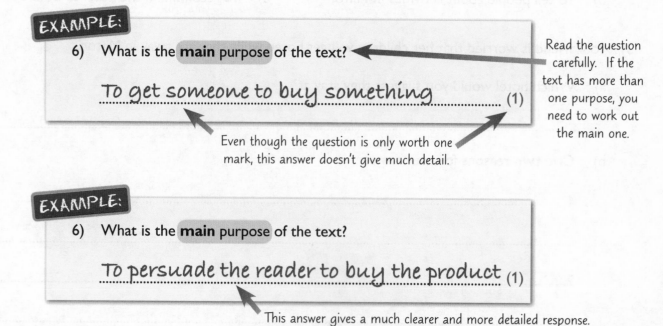

EXAMPLE:

6) What is the **main** purpose of the text?

   To get someone to buy something _____ (1)

Read the question carefully. If the text has more than one purpose, you need to work out the main one.

Even though the question is only worth one mark, this answer doesn't give much detail.

EXAMPLE:

6) What is the **main** purpose of the text?

   To persuade the reader to buy the product (1)

This answer gives a much clearer and more detailed response.

Different Types of Question

Some questions will be about vocabulary

1) You could be asked to **identify** words with **similar meanings**.

> **EXAMPLE:**
>
> 13) What informal phrase is used instead of 'refuse to tolerate'?
>
> <u>won't stand for it</u> .... (1)

2) You may be asked to **explain** what a word **suggests** or **implies**.

> **EXAMPLE:**
>
> 14) 'Greaves Airlines intends to launch a new fleet of "superplanes" in 2028.'
>
> Give **one** word or phrase to replace 'intends' without changing the meaning.
>
> <u>plans</u> .... (1)

You'll need to give a word or phrase that means the same as 'intends' in the context of the quote.

You might have to give evidence to support your answer

1) Some questions will expect you to find the answer **in the text**.

> **EXAMPLE:**
>
> 15) The writer of Text A thinks that progress has been **slow**.
> Give **one** word or phrase from the text that suggests this.
>
> <u>a snail's pace</u> .... (1)

2) If you're using a quotation, make sure you write down **exactly** what appears in the text.

3) You might also have to **compare** texts — make sure you use examples from **both** texts if you're asked to.

Turn to p.22 for advice on how to answer comparison questions.

> 16) Compare Text A **and** Text B.
>
> a) Give **one** idea that is different in Text A and Text B.
>
> b) Give **one** example from **both** Text A and Text B to support your answer to part (a).

The question is asking you to compare the two texts and give evidence to support your comparison.

The Reading Test

Reading Test Advice

Use your time sensibly

1) Before you start, check the front of your paper to see **how many marks** are available and **how much time** you have to write your answers.

2) **Divide your time sensibly** — spend **more time** on questions worth **more marks**.

3) If you're really **stuck** on a **multiple-choice question**, make a **sensible guess**.

Read every question carefully

The most important thing to remember is:

> Make sure you **answer the question**. Only pick out **relevant information**.

1) Check each question to make sure you're using the **correct text**.

2) This is especially important if you're **comparing more than one text**.

Make sure you give two clear differences between the opinions in the texts.

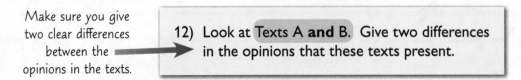

12) Look at Texts A **and** B. Give two differences in the opinions that these texts present.

3) Make sure **each point** you write is **separate** and you haven't put the **same thing twice**.

You're not marked on spelling, punctuation or grammar

1) In the **reading test**, you **don't** need to worry about **spelling**, **punctuation** or **grammar** unless you're specifically asked about it.

2) However, if you copy out **quotations** from a **text**, you need to spell them **correctly**.

3) Don't use your **dictionary** too much. Only use it if it will help you **answer** a question.

4) Answers **don't** have to be in **sentences**, but they must answer the **question** fully.

5) Make sure you pick out the **correct information** and that your answer is **clear**.

Prepare well for onscreen testing

1) If you're doing your test on a computer, try to do an **onscreen sample test** beforehand.

2) Make sure you know what all the **buttons** do and how the test **works**.

3) Ask your **teacher** or **tutor** for **more information** about what your test will be like.

Functional Skills

English　　　Level 1

Reading

Text Booklet

Time allowed: 60 minutes

Instructions to candidates
- All answers must be written in the Question Booklet.
- **Do not** write any answers inside this Text Booklet.

Information for candidates
- There are **two texts** in this booklet:
  Text A — internet forum discussion
  Text B — article
- You will be tested on **both** texts in the Question Booklet.

Advice for candidates
- Read each text carefully before you start answering the questions.

Text A

An internet forum discussion about Sunday opening hours.

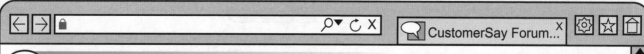

Customer Discussion Forum

| Post a reply | Start a new thread |

Should shops open later on Sundays?

 Jackie Athersmith New Member   Posted: 15th March 17:15

I am frustrated that shops don't open for a full day on Sundays. My local supermarket is only open from 10 am - 4 pm on Sundays, which is inconvenient for me and probably for many other people. I'm a busy mum of three and I work full-time as a nurse, so the only free time I have is on a Sunday evening. Ideally, that's when I would do my weekly food shop, but I can't. Larger supermarkets in Scotland are open 24 hours, 7 days a week, so clearly it is possible. Can someone explain the purpose of Sunday trading laws?

Re: Should shops open later on Sundays?

 Chen Zhao Forum Member   Posted: 16th March 10:26

I understand where you're coming from Jackie, but shopping hours are limited on Sundays for a reason. Sunday should be the day for spending quality time with your family. You can order your shopping online at any time and have it delivered to your house at a time that's convenient for you. That seems like the most straightforward solution to your problem. Plus, the cost of delivery is very cheap. Consider those people who'd have to work longer on Sundays if the law changed — I'm sure they'd prefer to spend some leisure time with friends and family rather than work until 9 pm on a Sunday evening!

Re: Should shops open later on Sundays?

 Joel Griffin Expert Forum Member   Posted: 16th March 12:43

Hi Jackie, here are some arguments for and against shorter Sunday trading hours:

For:

- It gives employees guaranteed time off

- If larger shops are open all the time, smaller shops may not be able to compete, and they could go out of business

Against:

- Staff could earn more money if they could work more hours

- Shops may have to employ additional staff, which could decrease unemployment rates

- According to the article here, 70% of people wish supermarkets were open longer

---

Related Discussions

- Why do shops have to close so early on Sundays?
- Why doesn't Scotland have restricted trading hours on Sundays?
- Can small shops open late on Sundays?

Contact Us | **Register** | **Forum Rules** | **Online Safety** | **Advertisers** | **Terms and Conditions**

Text B

An article giving advice about shopping online.

The Advice Centre

Shopping Safely Online

Author: Sana Ali

More than half of the adults in the UK now shop on the internet, and £1 in every £5 is spent online.

Internet shopping has transformed the way we shop. People are no longer restricted by shop opening hours, as online shopping lets you buy almost anything at any time, day or night. However, some people think that online shopping is risky. By asking yourself the following questions, you can make sure your online shopping experience is as safe and satisfactory as possible.

1. Am I getting the best price?

Shopping online lets you easily compare prices from a number of places without having to walk all over town. Always shop around to make sure the price you're paying is the best one. Look out for sales and special offers that can get you big discounts. Beware of prices that look too good to be true though — they usually are!

2. How much will delivery cost?

You might find what you're looking for at a really good price.

However, there is often a delivery charge to have the item sent to you. Delivery charges can be expensive, so make sure you check before buying anything to avoid a nasty surprise when you come to pay.

3. Are my details safe?

To buy something online, you'll usually pay using a credit or debit card. Before you enter your card details, always check that:

- the website address starts with https://

- there is a padlock symbol at the top of the screen, next to the address bar.

These tell you that the website is encrypted. If the padlock symbol is missing, your card details could be read by other parties that you haven't given permission to.

4. Can I return the item?

Many people believe that you can return any item for any reason, but this isn't always the case. Make sure to read the returns policy of the website you're buying from. All shops have to refund the cost of items that are faulty. Some shops might let you return something if you've just changed your mind, but others might not.

Remember: If you're not sure about a website, don't use it!

Candidate Surname	Candidate Forename(s)

Date	Candidate Signature

Functional Skills

English   Level 1

Reading
Question Booklet

Time allowed: 60 minutes

You **may** use a dictionary.

Instructions to candidates
- Use **black or blue ink** to write your answers.
- Write your name and the date in the spaces provided above.
- Read the Text Booklet provided.
- There are **3 sections** in this paper.
  Answer **all questions** in each section in the spaces provided.
- Cross through any work or planning you do not want to be marked.

Information for candidates
- There are **30 marks** available for this paper.
- There are **15 questions** in this paper.
- The marks available are given in brackets at the end of each question.
- You do not need to write full sentences in your answers.
- You will not be marked on spelling, punctuation or grammar.

Advice to candidates
- Make sure you understand each question before you start answering it.
- If you have time, check your answers at the end.

Total Marks

Answer every question. Write all answers in the spaces provided.

Section A

You'll need to read Text A to answer Questions 1 to 7.

1 What is the purpose of Joel Griffin's post on the forum?

   A To instruct Jackie on what she should do ☐

   B To inform Jackie about the different arguments relating to Sunday hours ☐

   C To persuade Jackie that shops should not open later ☐

   D To describe a shopping experience he has had ☐

[1 mark]

2 Using Text A, give **two** reasons why Jackie Athersmith can only go shopping on Sundays.

   Reason 1 ....

   Reason 2 ....

[2 marks]

3 Using Text A, write down **two** possible advantages of longer opening hours on Sundays.

   Advantage 1 ....

   ....

   Advantage 2 ....

   ....

[2 marks]

4   Using Text A, identify **two** possible reasons why Sunday opening hours should **not** be changed.

Reason 1 ....

....

Reason 2 ....

....

[2 marks]

5   You can use a dictionary for this question.

a) 'employ additional staff'

Suggest **one** word or phrase that could replace 'additional' without changing the meaning of the quotation.

....

[1 mark]

b) 'the most straightforward solution'

Suggest **one** word or phrase that could replace 'straightforward' without changing the meaning of the quotation.

....

[1 mark]

6   Identify **two** language features used in Text A.

Feature 1 ....

Feature 2 ....

[2 marks]

7   a)   In Chen Zhao's forum post, which phrase means 'time spent outside of work'?

....

[1 mark]

b)   In Joel Griffin's forum post, which phrase means 'to lower the number of people without jobs'?

....

[1 mark]

Total for Section A = 13 marks

[Turn over]

Section B

You'll need to read Text B to answer Questions 8 to 14.

8 Using Text B, tick the correct boxes to show whether each statement is a fact or an opinion.

	Fact	Opinion
You can compare prices online		
Online shopping is risky		
A padlock symbol tells you that a website is encrypted		
You can return any item for any reason		

[2 marks]

9 What information can you infer from the pictures in Text B?

Picture in paragraph 2:

....

....

Picture in paragraph 3:

....

....

[2 marks]

10 Identify **three** features used in Text B to organise the article's content.

Feature 1 ....

Feature 2 ....

Feature 3 ....

[3 marks]

11 Using Text B, identify **two** security measures to look for before sending your data to a website.

Measure 1 ....

....

Measure 2 ....

....

[2 marks]

12 'If you're not sure about a website, don't use it!'

Name and explain the effect of the final punctuation mark in this quotation from Text B.

Punctuation mark: ....

Effect: ....

....

[2 marks]

13 a) What is the purpose of Text B?

    A To persuade the reader to use encrypted websites ☐

    B To tell the reader how to save money online ☐

    C To advise the reader about shopping safely online ☐

    D To advise the reader about returning online purchases ☐

[1 mark]

b) Give **one** quotation from Text B that supports your answer.

....

....

[1 mark]

14 '**More than half**' and '**£1 in every £5**' are examples of

    A Formal language ☐

    B Statistics ☐

    C Opinions ☐

    D Exclamations ☐

[1 mark]

Total for Section B = 14 marks

Section C

You'll need to read Texts A to B to answer Question 15.

15 Text A and Text B both discuss shopping. Compare the main ideas in each text to find **two** similarities and **one** difference between them.

Similarity 1 ....

....

Similarity 2 ....

....

Difference ....

....

[3 marks]

Total for Section C = 3 marks

Total for paper = 30 marks

Knowing your Audience and Purpose

Audience and purpose are important

1) The **audience** is the **person** who reads a text.

2) You need to know **who** your audience is so that you know what **style** to write in.

3) The **purpose** is the **reason** a text is written. For example, to **explain** or **instruct**.

4) The purpose of a text tells you **what** to write about and **how** to write it.

Find out who you are writing for and why

The question will tell you **who** the text is for (audience) and **why** you are writing it (purpose).

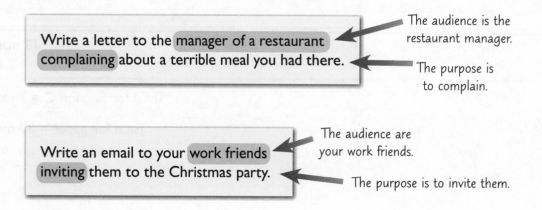

Write a letter to the manager of a restaurant complaining about a terrible meal you had there.

The audience is the restaurant manager.

The purpose is to complain.

Write an email to your work friends inviting them to the Christmas party.

The audience are your work friends.

The purpose is to invite them.

Use the correct writing style

Make sure the way you write **fits** the audience and the purpose.

See p.12 for more on style.

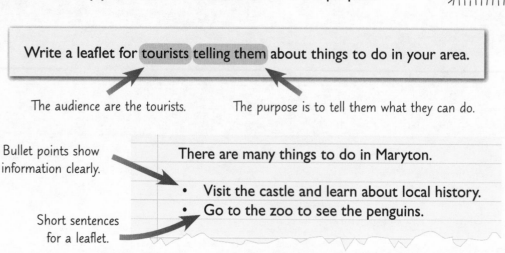

Write a leaflet for tourists telling them about things to do in your area.

The audience are the tourists.   The purpose is to tell them what they can do.

Bullet points show information clearly.

Short sentences for a leaflet.

There are many things to do in Maryton.

• Visit the castle and learn about local history.
• Go to the zoo to see the penguins.

Practice Questions

1) Write down the audience and purpose for each of these writing tasks.

   a) The boiler in your flat has broken. Write an email to your landlord asking him to fix it.

   Audience ....

   Purpose ....

   b) Write an email to your manager asking for time off work to go to the dentist.

   Audience ....

   Purpose ....

   c) Write a letter to the council asking them to fix the potholes on your road.

   Audience ....

   Purpose ....

   d) Write a letter applying for a job in a shop.

   Audience ....

   Purpose ....

   e) Write a newspaper article arguing that speed limits in town centres should be lower.

   Audience ....

   Purpose ....

2) Formal writing is for people you don't know or people in charge.
   Informal writing is for people you know well.

   What type of writing style would you use for these writing tasks? Circle 'Formal' or 'Informal'.

   a) A letter to your best friend describing your holiday   Formal / Informal

   b) An email to your manager about your annual review   Formal / Informal

   c) A letter of complaint to a bus company   Formal / Informal

   d) A thank you letter to your Gran for a birthday present   Formal / Informal

   e) An email to your bank manager about your overdraft   Formal / Informal

Planning your Answer

Make a plan before you start writing

1) Planning your answer will help you put your ideas **in order**.

2) Make sure you **only** write down points that **answer the question**.

3) Making a plan will help you give your answer a **clear** beginning, middle and end.

4) Some tests may give you **space** to plan your answer, but your plan **won't** be **marked**.

Write your plan using notes

1) Write your points down and give them an **order**.

2) For instructions, you should put your points in the **order** the reader needs to **do them**.

3) For other writing tasks, you should **organise** your points in order of **importance**.

> Write an email to your landlord telling him about the problems in your flat.

Most important point comes first. →
1) Boiler is broken — heating won't work
2) Kitchen tap drips
3) Stain on hall carpet

4) Using a **spider diagram** might help you see how points are **connected**.

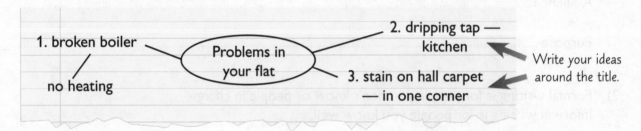

1. broken boiler
no heating

Problems in your flat

2. dripping tap — kitchen

3. stain on hall carpet — in one corner

Write your ideas around the title.

How to plan a letter

1) Work out who the audience is to help decide if the letter should be **formal** or **informal**.

2) This will help you decide which **greeting** and **ending** to use.

3) Your first paragraph should tell the reader the **purpose** of the letter.

4) The main body of the letter **develops** your ideas and gives more **detail**.

5) The last paragraph should tell the reader what **action** you want them to take.

See p.64 for more on letters.

Planning your Answer

How to plan an email

1) Think about **who** is going to read the email. This is your **audience**.

2) This will help you work out if your style should be **formal** or **informal**.

3) The **first point** in your plan should be the **purpose** of the email.

4) Write a **paragraph** in the email for **each** point in your plan.

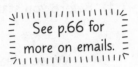

See p.66 for more on emails.

How to plan an article

Work out your **purpose** and **audience**. Think about **where** the article will be printed.

> Write an article for a charity newsletter about an upcoming fund raising activity.

The audience for this article will be a group of people — the charity members.

Start with the main facts. What happened, where, when and who?

Then go into detail about the event.

Audience: newsletter readers   Purpose: to explain

1) Sponsored hike / Mount Snowdon / 6th Aug / four of us
2) 35 km / raising money for hospice
3) Need £500 for new equipment

How to plan a report

The purpose of a report is to **give information**. It needs to be **clear** and **accurate**.

> Your co-worker has had an accident at work. Write a report for the Safety Officer telling them what happened.

Use formal language for reports.

Injury: broken leg, sprained wrist
Cause: ladder slipped, fell onto floor
Solution: safety ladder, signs, more training

Divide the information clearly into sections.

Planning your Answer

How to plan a leaflet

1) Before you start planning, think about what information the audience **needs**.

> Write a leaflet giving people advice on how to improve home security.

2) Start by telling the reader the **purpose** of the leaflet.

3) In your plan, write a **list** of points. Make sure they are **all** relevant.

4) **Number** your points in order from **most** to **least important**.

5) End with a **reminder** about **why** the audience needs to think about the subject.

How to plan a forum response or a review

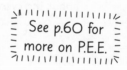

A forum is a web page where people discuss a particular subject.

1) The purpose of a forum response or a review is to **give** your **opinion** and **argue** a point.

2) Forum responses and reviews can also be used to **explain** something.

3) Your **first point** should clearly explain your main argument.

4) You'll get better marks if your **argument** is **balanced**.

5) Remember to include a point or two from the **other side** of the argument.

See p.60 for more on P.E.E.

6) The rest of your points should **back up** your **argument**. Use P.E.E.

7) Use **persuasive language** to convince people of your point of view.

How to fill in forms

1) Read the **instructions** before you start and make sure you **follow them**.

2) Carefully fill in **every part** of the form. Write 'n/a' if something doesn't apply to you.

3) If you are asked about your **education** or **jobs**, start with the **most recent** first.

4) For **longer answers**, write a **rough plan** before filling in the form.

Practice Question

1) You are working at a call centre for an internet company. There have been some complaints from customers about the way staff speak to them on the phone.

Write a leaflet giving advice to call centre staff about how to treat customers on the phone.

You should include advice about:

• what staff should do

• what staff should not do

• why it is important to deal with customers politely

Write your plan here. Remember to think about how to divide up the information.

Writing and Checking Your Answer

Use your plan to write your answer

1) Put the ideas in your plan into **full sentences**.

2) Group sentences about the **same thing** into paragraphs.

3) Use the same **order** and **structure** you decided on in your plan.

4) Make sure your writing style is right for your **audience and purpose**.

5) This answer is often called a **first draft**.

Improve your writing by checking it

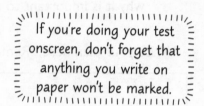

If you're doing your test onscreen, don't forget that anything you write on paper won't be marked.

1) Read over your answer carefully and **make improvements**.

2) Take out anything you **don't need**.

3) Add in extra details that **improve** your answer and make it **more interesting**.

4) Check that your **spelling, punctuation** and **grammar** are correct.

> Many street lights in your town are broken and have not been fixed.
> Write a letter to your local council asking them to improve street lighting.

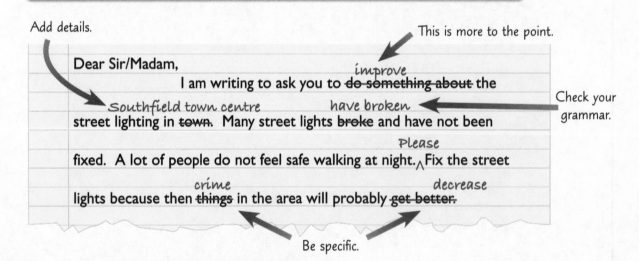

Add details.

This is more to the point.

Check your grammar.

Be specific.

Dear Sir/Madam,
I am writing to ask you to ~~do something about~~ *improve* the
street lighting in ~~town.~~ *Southfield town centre* Many street lights ~~broke~~ *have broken* and have not been
fixed. A lot of people do not feel safe walking at night. *Please* Fix the street
lights because then ~~things~~ *crime* in the area will probably ~~get better.~~ *decrease*

Write a final draft if you have time

1) Once you have **corrected** your first draft, you can write out a **final draft**.

2) **Keep track** of the **time** you have left. You might not have time for a final draft in the test.

3) Don't panic if you don't have time — just make sure that any **corrections** you've written are **clear enough** for the examiner to understand.

4) Drafting is often used in more **formal situations**, like when you're writing a **report** at work.

Practice Question

1) Here is a writing task and an example plan for an answer.

> You are organising a surprise party for your sister's 21st birthday.
> Write an email to her friends inviting them to the party.

<u>Audience</u>: sister's friends (informal)   <u>Purpose</u>: invite / inform

<u>Details</u>
- What: 21st birthday party for Sarah, pirate theme
- When: March 25th — early until late
- Where: Brinton village hall — directions / take bus no.34

<u>Anything else</u>
- Costumes / bring themed food and drink
- Other friends welcome
- Keep secret — let me know response by next Friday

Turn this plan into a first draft. Make improvements and add details as you write.

....

....

....

....

....

....

....

....

....

....

....

....

Using Paragraphs

Paragraphs make writing easier to read

1) A paragraph is a **group of sentences**.

2) These sentences talk about the **same thing** or **follow on** from each other.

Divide your plan into paragraphs

1) Give each **point** in your plan its own **paragraph**.

2) Start with an **introduction** paragraph. It should **summarise** what your answer is about.

3) Make your last paragraph a **conclusion**. It should **sum up** your main point.

Use paragraphs to show when something changes

1) Start a new paragraph when you talk about a different **topic, person, place** or **time**.

2) To show a new paragraph start a **new line**.

You can leave a space to show it's a new paragraph.

Different people.

Different place.

Start a new paragraph on a new line.

> Residents in Newton were woken yesterday morning by loud explosions.
> Police arrived to find smoke coming from a local industrial estate. Police dogs were called in to search the area.
> In a warehouse in the far corner of the estate, officers found a mountain of fireworks.

Use P.E.E. to develop your points

P.E.E. stands for **Point, Example, Explanation**. It helps to **structure** your paragraphs.

Make your point first.

Give an example to support your point.

> Riding a bike without a helmet is dangerous. Last week, a cyclist without a helmet was badly injured when they hit a car. Doctors said that their injuries would have been much less serious if they had been wearing a helmet.

Explain how the example backs up your point.

Practice Question

1) Read this piece of writing about Glastonbury music festival.
   Rewrite it underneath with new paragraphs in the correct places.

> Glastonbury festival is a big music and arts event held in Somerset. Some of the most successful pop artists in history, such as Oasis, U2 and Coldplay, have played there. The festival began in the 1970s and was organised by locals. When a farmer, called Michael Eavis, took over the organisation of the festival, it began to grow in size. Now the festival is held every year, although occasionally there is a break which allows the fields to recover. This means that the fields can still be used for farming. Glastonbury is not just a music festival. It hosts many dance, comedy and theatre acts. There are also sculptures and works of art around the site.

....

....

....

....

....

....

....

....

....

....

....

....

....

Changing your Layout

Layout is a way of making writing interesting

1) Some texts use **layout** to **organise** information.

2) An interesting layout can make the **important points** stand out.

3) It also helps to make a piece of writing **clear** and **easy to read**.

Make sure your layout fits the question

For **articles**, **leaflets** and **reports** think about using different layouts:

> Write a leaflet telling people about electric cars. You should talk about the advantages and disadvantages of electric cars.

1) Use **headings** and **subheadings** to give a **clear structure**.

2) The **main heading** tells you what the whole text is about.

3) **Subheadings** break the writing into smaller sections.

4) They tell the reader what **each part** is about.

5) Use **bullet points** or **numbers** for **lists** because they are easy to follow.

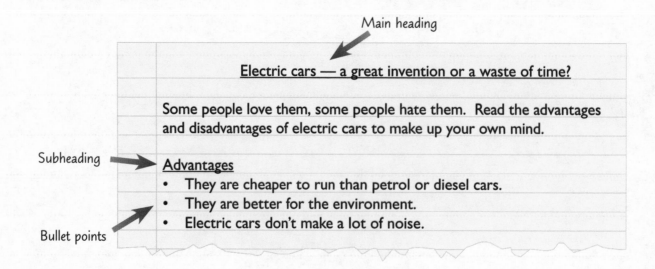

Main heading

Electric cars — a great invention or a waste of time?

Some people love them, some people hate them. Read the advantages and disadvantages of electric cars to make up your own mind.

Subheading → Advantages
- They are cheaper to run than petrol or diesel cars.
Bullet points → • They are better for the environment.
- Electric cars don't make a lot of noise.

Practice Question

1) You have recently started working at a tourist information office.
   They have asked you to write a report about the sports facilities in your town.

   You should write about:

   • what sports facilities there are

   • who uses the facilities

   • what sports facilities you think the town needs

   Remember to use your layout to organise the information in your report.

   ....

   ....

   ....

   ....

   ....

   ....

   ....

   ....

   ....

   ....

   ....

   ....

   ....

   ....

   ....

   ....

   ....

   ....

Writing Letters

Formal letters are for people you don't know

1) Start with a **formal greeting**. For example, 'Dear Sir / Madam' or 'Dear Mr Jones'.

2) **End** with 'Yours sincerely' if you know their name or 'Yours faithfully' if you don't.

3) Avoid **slang** and **exclamation marks**.

Informal letters are for people you know well

1) Start with the reader's **name**. End with 'Best wishes' or 'See you soon'.

2) You can be more **chatty** but make sure your spelling and grammar are correct.

Follow the rules for writing letters

There are some things that all **formal letters** need.

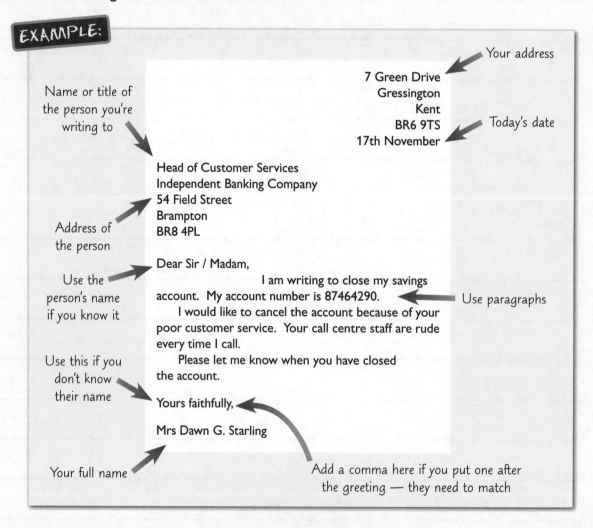

EXAMPLE:

Your address

Name or title of the person you're writing to

Today's date

Address of the person

Use the person's name if you know it

Use paragraphs

Use this if you don't know their name

Your full name

Add a comma here if you put one after the greeting — they need to match

7 Green Drive
Gressington
Kent
BR6 9TS
17th November

Head of Customer Services
Independent Banking Company
54 Field Street
Brampton
BR8 4PL

Dear Sir / Madam,

I am writing to close my savings account. My account number is 87464290.

I would like to cancel the account because of your poor customer service. Your call centre staff are rude every time I call.

Please let me know when you have closed the account.

Yours faithfully,

Mrs Dawn G. Starling

Practice Question

1) Write a letter applying for the job described below. Make sure your layout is correct.

> Food Xpress is looking for staff to work on the tills in their new supermarket.
> Staff must be over 16, friendly and hard-working.
> If you would like to apply, please write to the Store Manager, Mr Simon Green.
> The address is Food Xpress, 17 Park Road, Middleton, Surrey, KT8 7MF.

You should include:

- why you would like the job

- why you're a suitable applicant

Writing Emails

Email is electronic mail

1) Email is a way of sending **messages** from one computer to another.

2) You send them to a person's or company's **email address**.

tedsmith@tedstravel.co.uk

← The bit before the '@' sign is usually the person's name or title.

Lay out emails correctly

All emails have certain **features**. Make sure you include all the right information.

EXAMPLE:

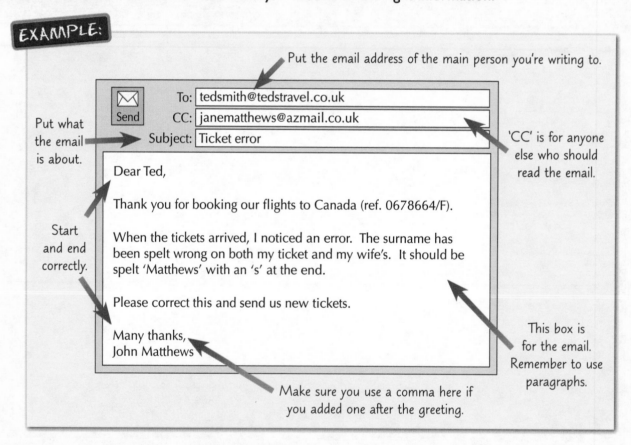

Put the email address of the main person you're writing to.

	To:	tedsmith@tedstravel.co.uk
Send	CC:	janematthews@azmail.co.uk
	Subject:	Ticket error

Put what the email is about.

'CC' is for anyone else who should read the email.

Dear Ted,

Thank you for booking our flights to Canada (ref. 0678664/F).

When the tickets arrived, I noticed an error. The surname has been spelt wrong on both my ticket and my wife's. It should be spelt 'Matthews' with an 's' at the end.

Please correct this and send us new tickets.

Many thanks,
John Matthews

Start and end correctly.

This box is for the email. Remember to use paragraphs.

Make sure you use a comma here if you added one after the greeting.

Check that your style is right for the audience

1) When you email a **company** or a **person in charge**, use **formal** language.

2) Emails to **family** and **friends** can be more **informal**.

Practice Question

1) Read this email from a co-worker about a sponsored walk.

Reply	From: karlie.grey@azmail.co.uk
	To: companyworkers@azmail.co.uk
	Subject: Sponsored walk

Hello everyone,

I'm doing a sponsored walk on Saturday in the Lake District. The walk is 25 miles long and hilly! I'm walking to raise money for St Mary's Hospital. Can you sponsor me? If you can, let me know how much you would like to give.

Also, does anyone want to join me? Let me know if you do.

Thanks,
Karlie

Write a short reply which says:

- how much money you would like to offer Karlie

- that you would like to join the walk

- why the sponsored walk is a good idea

Send	To: karlie.grey@azmail.co.uk
	CC: companyworkers@azmail.co.uk
	Subject: Sponsored walk

....

....

....

....

....

....

....

Parts of a Sentence

Always write in sentences

1) You **don't** need to use full sentences in your **plan**. Use notes instead.

2) You **do** get marks for using **full sentences** in writing exercises.

3) Turn your notes into **full sentences** when you write your answer.

A sentence must make sense on its own

1) Every sentence needs an **action word** and **somebody** to do it.

2) A verb is an action word. It tells you **what happens** in a sentence.

Every morning my neighbour **runs** to work.   This is the verb.

3) A sentence needs **someone** or **something** to 'do' the verb.

The machine is 'doing' the action.

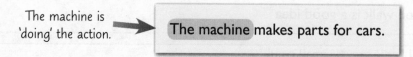

The machine makes parts for cars.

4) Sentences can also show **who** or **what** an action is being done to.

I sold my **coin collection.**   The selling was 'done' to the coin collection.

Check you have used the right article

1) **Articles** go **before nouns** and give you **more information** about the noun.

2) There are **two types** of article.

3) 'a' and 'an' are used for **general** things. Only use 'an' when the noun starts with a **vowel sound**.

She wants **a** lemon.   She wants any lemon. He wants any orange.   He wants **an** orange.   'orange' starts with a vowel sound, so use 'an'.

4) 'the' is used for **specific** things.

He wants **the** pear.   He wants a specific pear.

Parts of a Sentence

Form sentences by putting all the parts together

Put the article, the person or thing **doing** the action, and the **verb** together.

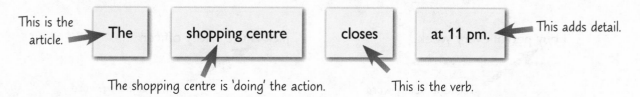

This is the article. → **The** **shopping centre** **closes** **at 11 pm.** ← This adds detail.

The shopping centre is 'doing' the action.   This is the verb.

Practice Questions

1) Underline the verb in each sentence.

a) We both applied for the same job.

b) All of our staff wear uniforms.

c) Everyone left the building at lunchtime.

d) I passed my driving test last year.

2) Underline who or what is doing the action.

a) Sometimes dogs howl at the moon.

b) Your car makes a strange noise.

c) The leisure centre opens at 10 am.

d) The manager gave me a pay rise.

3) Read these notes from a staff room notice board. Rewrite the notes in full sentences.

> thefts in staff room last week
> take care of belongings
> mobile phones and wallets — in your locker
> if anything missing let manager know

....

....

....

....

....

....

Talking About Things in the Present

A verb is a 'doing' or 'being' word

Use verbs to describe what something **does** or **is**.

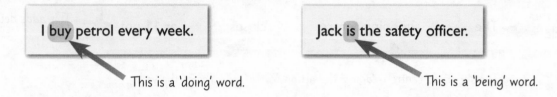

I buy petrol every week.

This is a 'doing' word.

Jack is the safety officer.

This is a 'being' word.

Use the present tense to say what is happening now

Most verbs in the **present tense** follow the same **verb pattern**:

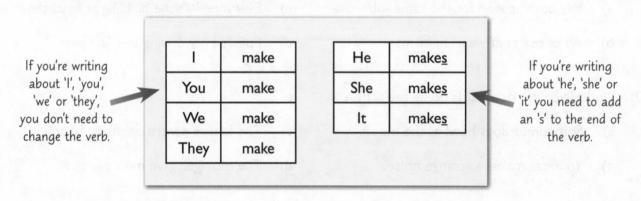

If you're writing about 'I', 'you', 'we' or 'they', you don't need to change the verb.

I	make
You	make
We	make
They	make

He	makes
She	makes
It	makes

If you're writing about 'he', 'she' or 'it' you need to add an 's' to the end of the verb.

How you change the verb depends on who is doing it

Use the **verb pattern** to work out the correct ending.

I make the bed.

The verb table shows that you don't need to change the verb when you're writing about 'I'.

She makes cupcakes.

You need to add an 's' to the verb because you're talking about 'she'.

They sell bicycles.

You don't need to change the verb when you're writing about 'they'.

It sells furniture.

You need to add an 's' to the verb because you're talking about 'it'.

Talking About Things in the Past

Use the past tense to say what has already happened

1) For most verbs you need to add '**ed**' to the end to make them past tense.

2) If the verb already ends in '**e**', just add a '**d**' to the end.

Not all past tense verbs add 'ed'

You need to learn these exceptions.

1) Some verbs follow their own **patterns**.

Verb	Past Tense
I do	I did
I have	I had
I see	I saw
I get	I got
I take	I took

Verb	Past Tense
I am / We are	I was / We were
I go	I went
I make	I made
I come	I came
I think	I thought

Use 'was' for 'I', 'he', 'she' and 'it'. Use 'were' for 'you', 'we' and 'they'.

These are just a few examples. There are other verbs that act differently too.

2) Some verbs **don't change** at all in the past tense:

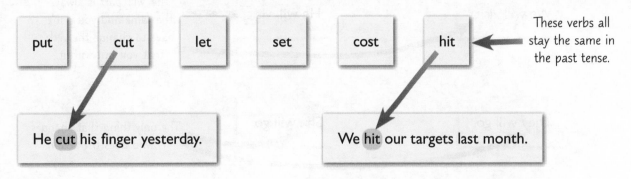

put   cut   let   set   cost   hit

These verbs all stay the same in the past tense.

He cut his finger yesterday.

We hit our targets last month.

Talking About Things in the Future

To talk about the future you can use 'I am going'...

1) Talk about future actions by using the correct version of '**I am going**'.

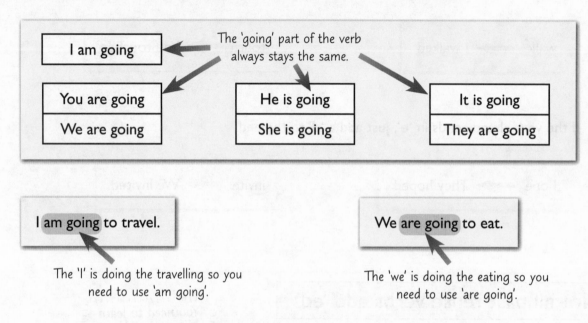

The 'going' part of the verb always stays the same.

| I am going |
| You are going |
| We are going |
| He is going |
| She is going |
| It is going |
| They are going |

I am going to travel.

The 'I' is doing the travelling so you need to use 'am going'.

We are going to eat.

The 'we' is doing the eating so you need to use 'are going'.

2) You need to put the word '**to**' **in front** of the action being done.

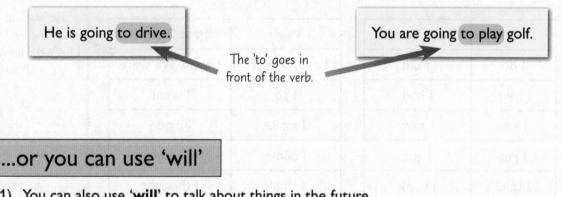

He is going to drive.

You are going to play golf.

The 'to' goes in front of the verb.

...or you can use 'will'

1) You can also use '**will**' to talk about things in the future.

2) The 'will' part **never changes**. It doesn't matter **who** is doing the action.

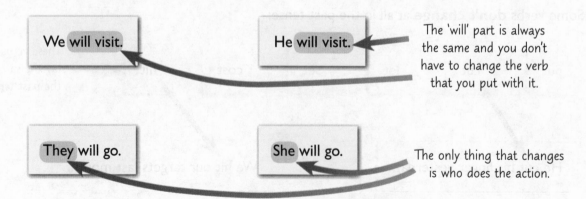

We will visit.

He will visit.

The 'will' part is always the same and you don't have to change the verb that you put with it.

They will go.

She will go.

The only thing that changes is who does the action.

Using Tenses Consistently

Stay in the same tense in your writing

1) All the verbs in your writing need to be **consistent** with each other.

2) This means verbs that are in the **same sentence** usually need to be in the **same tense**.

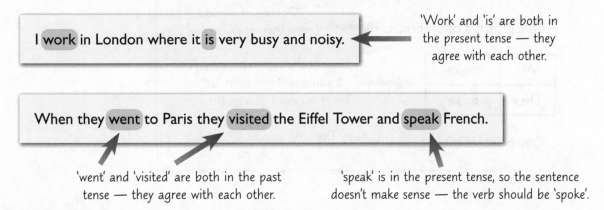

I work in London where it is very busy and noisy.

'Work' and 'is' are both in the present tense — they agree with each other.

When they went to Paris they visited the Eiffel Tower and speak French.

'went' and 'visited' are both in the past tense — they agree with each other.

'speak' is in the present tense, so the sentence doesn't make sense — the verb should be 'spoke'.

Practice Questions

1) Rewrite the following sentences to talk about the time in brackets.

a) Brian carries a briefcase. (the past)

....

b) I applied for a driving licence. (the future)

....

c) My friend lived in Brighton. (the present)

....

d) We do the washing up. (the past)

....

2) Underline the incorrect verb in each sentence, and then rewrite the verbs using the time in brackets.

a) My car broke down when I drive to work. (the past) ....

b) The boss will get angry if you were late. (the future) ....

c) Belinda gets up and cycling to work. (the present) ....

d) I will go to Germany and I spoke German. (the past) ....

Common Mistakes with Verbs

A verb must match the person doing the action

Check **how many people** are doing the action to work out if the **verb** should **change**.

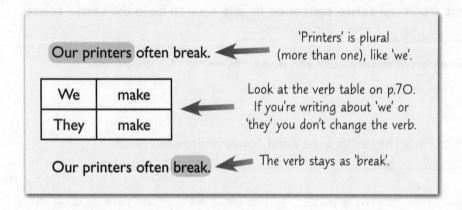

Our printers often break. ← 'Printers' is plural (more than one), like 'we'.

We	make
They	make

← Look at the verb table on p.70. If you're writing about 'we' or 'they' you don't change the verb.

Our printers often break. ← The verb stays as 'break'.

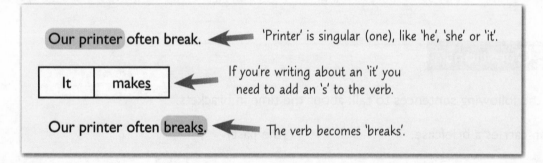

Our printer often break. ← 'Printer' is singular (one), like 'he', 'she' or 'it'.

It	make**s**

← If you're writing about an 'it' you need to add an 's' to the verb.

Our printer often breaks. ← The verb becomes 'breaks'.

Use the right 'being' word to go with the person

1) To say 'there **is**' or 'there **are**', use the right '**being**' word to match the person.

2) Use '**is**' when you're talking about **one person** or **thing**.
Use '**are**' when you're talking about **more than one** person or thing.

There is one security guard.

There are two security guards.

There is one security guard so use 'is'.

There are two security guards so use 'are'.

'Been' and 'done' always go with 'have' or 'has'

Always use '**have**' or '**has**' when you write 'been' or 'done'.

I have done the report you asked for.

You can't miss out the 'have' part. 'I done' doesn't make sense.

Common Mistakes with Verbs

Don't confuse 'could've' and 'could of'

1) Always write '**could have**'. Never write 'could of' because it doesn't mean anything.

2) It's the same for '**might have**' and '**should have**'.

He could have cleaned the house. I should have told him to.

It's always 'could have'. You can't say 'could of' or 'could has'.

Practice Questions

1) The verb in each sentence is wrong. Rewrite the sentence so the verb matches the person.
   Use the present tense.

   a) The women chats to the receptionist.

   ....

   b) Our dogs likes swimming.

   ....

   c) There are just one problem.

   ....

2) Rewrite each sentence so that it makes sense.

   a) We could of tried harder to arrive on time.

   ....

   b) The bank should of told us about the charges.

   ....

   c) I might of lost the key to the filing cabinet.

   ....

Using Joining Words

Joining words develop your writing

1) **Joining words connect** parts of sentences **together**.

2) You can use these words to join two **separate sentences** together:

for	and	nor	but	or	yet	so

Dani likes lamb. Ellie is a vegetarian. ➡️ Dani likes lamb, but Ellie is a vegetarian.

3) You can use these words to join the **main part** of a sentence to a **less important** part:

until	although	if	because	while	after

You can't go to the beach until I say so. ⬅️ 'until I say so' is just an extra detail and doesn't make sense on its own.

4) Using joining words in sentences will make your writing **more interesting**.

5) This will help you **pick up marks** in your writing test.

6) Don't **overuse** them though — too many can make your sentences long and difficult to follow.

'And', 'because' and 'so' add another point

Use '**and**', '**because**' or '**so**' to add **more detail** to a sentence.

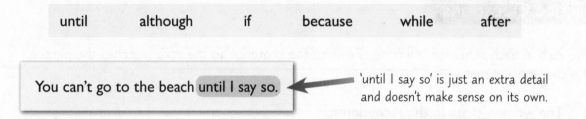

I run and cycle because I need to keep fit.

Sam is dieting so he can't eat fatty foods.

'because' and 'so' introduce explanations.

'But' and 'or' disagree with a point

1) Use '**but**' to **disagree** with something that's just been said.

Marcus is usually late but he arrived early today.

2) Use '**or**' to give an **alternative**.

We could go clubbing tonight or we could go bowling.

Practice Questions

1) Choose 'for', 'and', 'nor', 'but', 'or', 'yet' or 'so' to complete these sentences. Use each one once.

   a) You can sweeten this with either sugar .... jam.

   b) The shop will be closed on both Monday .... Tuesday.

   c) I drank a bottle of water .... I was incredibly thirsty.

   d) My aerobics class is cancelled .... I can come to the cinema.

   e) I wanted to walk the dog today .... it looks like it might rain.

   f) He doesn't like washing his car .... does he do a good job when he does wash it.

   g) It was very late at night .... we were wide awake.

2) Your cousin has invited you to her wedding ceremony and reception on 28th September.
The wedding is at 2 pm and the reception is at 7 pm. You are working until 6.30 pm on
that date. Your friend has offered to drive you to the reception after work.

Write a short reply to your cousin, explaining why you can only attend the reception.
Use the joining words 'so', 'because', 'while', 'after' and 'but'. You don't need to worry about layout.

....

....

....

....

....

....

....

....

....

....

Punctuating Sentences

Sentences start with capital letters...

Every sentence should begin with a **capital letter**.

The price of petrol keeps on rising.

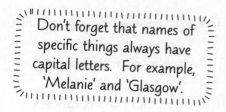

Don't forget that names of specific things always have capital letters. For example, 'Melanie' and 'Glasgow'.

...and end with full stops.

1) Use a **full stop** to show that your sentence has **finished**.

You need a full stop and a capital letter every time you finish one sentence and start another.

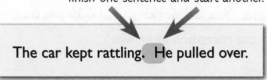

The car kept rattling. He pulled over.

2) Sometimes you might want to use an **exclamation mark instead** of a full stop.

3) **Only** use an exclamation mark if you're saying something really **amazing**.

I realised the exhaust had fallen off!   This exclamation mark shows shock and surprise.

4) Most sentences aren't amazing, so don't use too many exclamation marks.

5) If you're not sure, use a **full stop instead**.

Questions end with question marks

1) A question should **start** with a **capital letter** like a normal sentence.

2) You should **always end** a question with a **question mark** instead of a full stop.

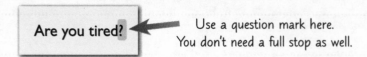

Are you tired?   Use a question mark here.
You don't need a full stop as well.

Practice Questions

1) Use capital letters and full stops to write these sentences correctly.
   You might need to write two sentences instead of one.

   a) She used to go to Cumbria every year

   ....

   b) they only like going on holiday in Britain

   ....

   c) please tell me what your favourite holiday was

   ....

   d) I said that i prefer Wales it never rains there

   ....

   e) we always go to Scotland on holiday it's really warm in the summer

   ....

   ....

   f) My favourite holiday was a trip to Malta it felt like home except it was much hotter

   ....

   ....

2) Use a full stop (.), exclamation mark (!) or question mark (?) to end each sentence correctly.

   a) It's rained for fifteen straight hours, I can't believe it's still raining...

   b) How often does it rain in London...

   c) The rainfall in Cornwall was about average this summer...

   d) It rained so much that I woke up one morning to find the kitchen flooded...

   e) Did you know it was the wettest summer on record...

   f) I think you'll find that it was the second wettest summer...

   g) Have you seen the weather report for next weekend...

Using Commas and Apostrophes

Commas separate things in a list

1) **Commas** can **break up lists** of **three** or **more** things.

2) Put a **comma** after **each thing** in the list.

3) Between the **last two things** you **don't** need a **comma**. Use '**and**' or '**or**' instead.

Commas split up the list
so it's easier to read.

You don't need a comma here.

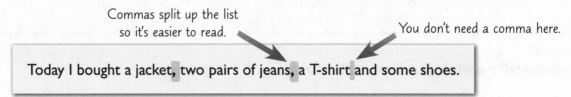

Today I bought a jacket, two pairs of jeans, a T-shirt and some shoes.

Apostrophes can show that letters are missing

1) An **apostrophe** looks like this — **'**

2) Apostrophes show where letters have been **removed** when joining two words together.

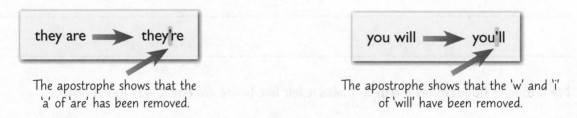

they are ➡ they're

The apostrophe shows that the
'a' of 'are' has been removed.

you will ➡ you'll

The apostrophe shows that the 'w' and 'i'
of 'will' have been removed.

'It's' and 'its' mean different things

1) '**It's**' means 'it is' or 'it has'.

2) The **apostrophe** shows that there are **letters missing**.

The apostrophe
shows that the 'i' is
missing from 'is'.

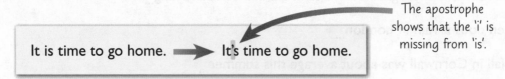

It is time to go home. ➡ It's time to go home.

3) '**Its**' means 'belonging to something or someone'.

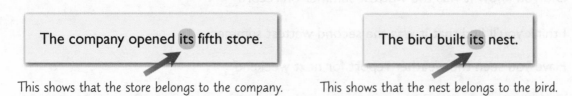

The company opened its fifth store.

This shows that the store belongs to the company.

The bird built its nest.

This shows that the nest belongs to the bird.

Using Commas and Apostrophes

Apostrophes can show who owns something

1) Add an **apostrophe** and '**s**' to show that something belongs to someone.

> Dev's cat jumped down from the tree.

2) If a plural ends in '**s**', you just need to add an **apostrophe** to the end of the word.

> The buses' schedules are new.

3) If a plural **doesn't** end in '**s**', you should add an **apostrophe** and '**s**'.

> The men's toilets are locked.

Practice Questions

1) Rewrite this sentence correctly by putting a comma in the correct place.

I want to paint my living room either yellow cream or ivory.

....

....

2) Shorten these phrases by putting apostrophes in the correct places.

a) they have ....   c) you are ....

b) cannot ....   d) I am ....

3) Circle the correct word to use in each sentence.

a) The team cancelled **it's / its** party.   b) Fry the chicken until **it's / its** golden.

4) Add an apostrophe and an 's' to the sentence below to show ownership.

She did not want to go to Aminta party.

....

Helpful Spelling Tips

The 'i' before 'e' rule

1) 'i' and 'e' often appear **next to each other** in a word.

2) This means it can be **tricky** to **remember** which comes **first**.

3) Use the **'i' before 'e' rule** to help:

'i' before 'e' except after 'c', but only when it rhymes with 'bee'.

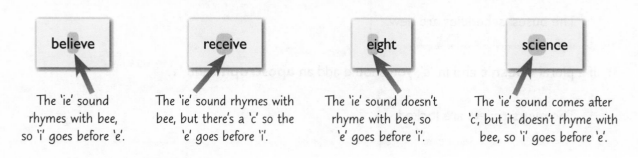

believe	receive	eight	science
The 'ie' sound rhymes with bee, so 'i' goes before 'e'.	The 'ie' sound rhymes with bee, but there's a 'c' so the 'e' goes before 'i'.	The 'ie' sound doesn't rhyme with bee, so 'e' goes before 'i'.	The 'ie' sound comes after 'c', but it doesn't rhyme with bee, so 'i' goes before 'e'.

A few words don't follow the rule

Watch out for these **tricky examples**.

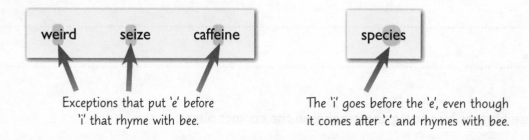

weird   seize   caffeine

Exceptions that put 'e' before 'i' that rhyme with bee.

species

The 'i' goes before the 'e', even though it comes after 'c' and rhymes with bee.

Use funny phrases to help you spell tricky words

Make up **sentences** or **phrases** to remind you how words are spelt.

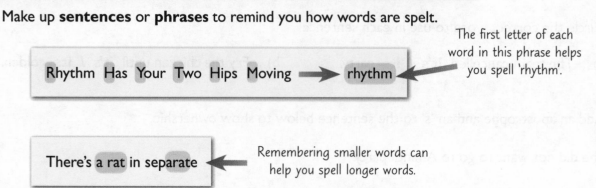

Rhythm Has Your Two Hips Moving ⟶ rhythm

The first letter of each word in this phrase helps you spell 'rhythm'.

There's a rat in separate

Remembering smaller words can help you spell longer words.

Practice Questions

1) Rewrite each word so it is spelt correctly. Some words may already be correct.

a) theif .... d) wierd ....

b) neighbour .... e) piece ....

c) cieling .... f) reciept ....

2) Think of four words that you find tricky to spell. Look up the spelling of each word in a dictionary and write it in the box. Think of a phrase to help you remember how to spell it.

....

....

....

....

....

....

....

Making Plurals

Plural means 'more than one'

1) To make most words **plural** you add an '**s**' on the **end**. For example, 'car' becomes 'cars'.

2) If a word **ends** with '**ch**', '**x**', '**s**', '**sh**' or '**z**', put '**es**' on the **end** to make it plural.

| two churches | some boxes | many dresses | three wishes | the waltzes |

Words ending with 'y' have different rules

1) Some words end with a **vowel** ('a', 'e', 'i', 'o' or 'u') and then a '**y**' (for example **boy**).

2) To make these words **plural**, put an '**s**' on the end. For example, 'key' becomes 'keys'.

3) Some words end with a **consonant** (any letter that isn't a **vowel**) and then a '**y**'.

4) To make them **plural**, change the '**y**' to an '**i**' and then add '**es**' on the **end**.

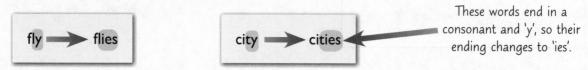

These words end in a consonant and 'y', so their ending changes to 'ies'.

Words ending with 'f' or 'fe' need a 'v'

1) Words ending in '**f**' can be made **plural** by changing the '**f**' to a '**v**' and adding '**es**'.

2) To make words ending with '**fe**' **plural**, change the '**f**' to a '**v**' and add '**s**'.

Making Plurals

Some words don't follow a pattern

1) To make some words **plural**, you have to change the **spelling** of the word.

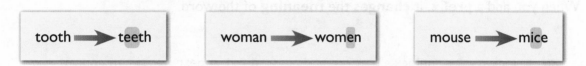

tooth ➡ teeth   woman ➡ women   mouse ➡ mice

2) Some words **don't change at all**.

fish   deer   sheep

You would always say 'two sheep', never 'two sheeps'.

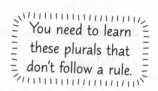

You need to learn these plurals that don't follow a rule.

Practice Questions

1) Write the plural of each word.

a) comb ....

d) duty ....

b) life ....

e) watch ....

c) fox ....

f) moose ....

2) Rewrite each of these sentences with the correct plurals.

a) The caterers need six loafs for the partys.

....

b) The shop sells penknifes and torchs.

....

c) Please give these ladys their room keies.

....

d) There are a few beachs close to the hoteles.

....

Adding Prefixes and Suffixes

Prefixes and suffixes are used to make new words

1) **Prefixes** are **letters** that are added to the **start** of words.

2) When you add a **prefix**, it **changes** the **meaning** of the word.

3) **Suffixes** are letters that are added to the **end** of words.

4) When you add a **suffix**, it also **changes** the **meaning** of the word.

 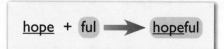

Adding a prefix doesn't change the spelling

If you add a **prefix** to a word, the **spelling** of the **word stays the same**.

The spelling of the prefix and the word don't change.

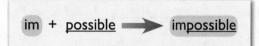

Adding a suffix might change the spelling

1) If you add a **suffix** to a word, sometimes the spelling **changes**.

2) If a word ends in an '**e**' and the **first letter** of the suffix is a **vowel**, you **drop** the '**e**'.

The vowels are 'a', 'e', 'i', 'o' and 'u'.

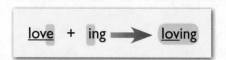 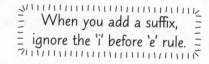

3) Some words end with a **consonant** and then a '**y**'.

4) When you add a **suffix** to these words, change the '**y**' to an '**i**'.

When you add a suffix, ignore the 'i' before 'e' rule.

Adding Prefixes and Suffixes

The C-V-C rule tells you when to double letters

1) If you are adding a **suffix** that begins with a **vowel**, you can use the **C-V-C rule**.

2) For most words, if the last three letters go **consonant - vowel - consonant (C-V-C)**...

All these words end with C-V-C.

3) ...you **double** the **last letter** when you add the **suffix**.

'ing' starts with a vowel, so double the 't'.

4) If the **first letter** of the **suffix** is a **consonant**, you **don't** double the last letter.

'ness' starts with a consonant, so don't double the 't'.

Practice Questions

1) Rewrite each word so it is spelt correctly. Some words may already be correct.

a) disgracful ....   d) regreted ....

b) happier ....   e) beting ....

c) fatter ....   f) cleverley ....

2) Rewrite each of these sentences and correct the mistakes.

a) He was takeing his brother to a writting class.

....

b) It's unnlucky that he's missplaced the ticket.

....

c) She dissagreed that I'd mispent my youth.

....

Common Spelling Mistakes

Words with double letters can be hard to spell

1) It's tricky to spell words with **double letters** because you **can't hear them** when they're said.

2) **Learn** how to spell these **common** words with **double letters**.

different   tomorrow   professional   address

Some words have more than one double letter.

necessary   immediate   occasionally   success

Silent letters and unclear sounds can be tricky

1) Sometimes you **can't hear** a certain **letter** when you say a word.

2) These are known as **silent letters**.

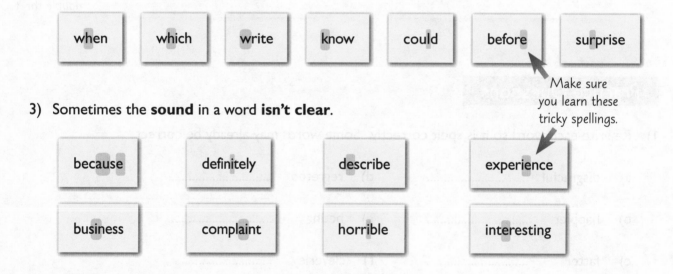

when   which   write   know   could   before   surprise

Make sure you learn these tricky spellings.

3) Sometimes the **sound** in a word **isn't clear**.

because   definitely   describe   experience

business   complaint   horrible   interesting

Make sure you're using the right word

1) '**A lot**' means '**many**'. '**Alot**' is **not** a word.

2) '**Thank you**' is always written as **two words**.

3) '**Maybe**' means '**perhaps**'. '**May be**' means '**might be**'.

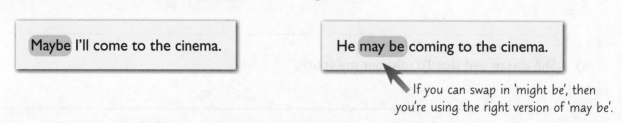

Maybe I'll come to the cinema.   He may be coming to the cinema.

If you can swap in 'might be', then you're using the right version of 'may be'.

Common Spelling Mistakes

Spell specialist words in full

1) Many specialist words are often **shortened**.

2) Make sure you can spell the **full word** so you can use it in **formal writing**.

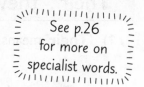
See p.26 for more on specialist words.

exam ➡ examination

ad ➡ advertisement

3) Specialist words can also be quite **tricky** to spell — here are some things to look out for:

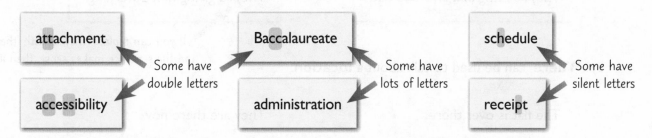

attachment

accessibility

Some have double letters

Baccalaureate

administration

Some have lots of letters

schedule

receipt

Some have silent letters

Practice Question

1) Each of these sentences has a mistake. Correct the mistake and rewrite the sentence.

a) Alot of people think fox-hunting is wrong.

....

b) He maybe catching an earlier flight.

....

c) I suprised my mum with a bunch of flowers.

....

d) Is Maxine definately going on maternity leave?

....

e) Owning a car is unecessary if you live in a city.

....

f) The eficiency of her work earned her a promotion.

....

Commonly Confused Words

'Their', 'they're' and 'there' are all different

1) **'Their'** means 'belonging to them'.

> Their flat has two bedrooms.

> He took their warning seriously.

2) **'They're'** means 'they are'.

> They're living in a two-bed flat.

> They're giving him a warning.

If you can replace 'they're' with 'they are', and the sentence makes sense, then it's right.

3) **'There'** can be used to talk about a **location**.

> The flat is over there.

> They are there now.

4) **'There'** can also **introduce a sentence**.

> There are two choices.

> There is no reason to give him a warning.

Learn how to use 'to' and 'too'

1) **'To'** can mean 'towards' or it can be part of a **verb**.

> He's going to Spain.

When 'to' means 'towards', it's followed by a place or an event.

> Tell him to meet me at 7 pm.

'To' is often followed by a verb.

2) **'Too'** can mean 'too much' or it can mean 'also'.

> This soup is too hot.

When 'too' means 'too much', it often has a describing word after it.

> She's going to the gig too.

When 'too' means 'also', it usually comes at the end of a sentence.

Commonly Confused Words

'You're' and 'your' mean different things

1) **'You're'** means 'you are'.

If you can replace 'you're' with 'you are' and the sentence makes sense, then it's the right word.

You're working twice this week.

2) **'Your'** means 'belonging to you'.

Keep your uniform in your locker.

The uniform belongs to you.

Don't confuse 'off' and 'of'

1) **'Off'** can mean 'not on'. **'Off'** can also mean 'away (from)'.

Turn the lights off.

I took Monday off work.

2) **'Of'** is a **linking word**. It **joins parts** of a sentence **together**.

My wardrobe is full of clothes I don't wear.

'Are' and 'our' sound alike

1) **'Are'** is a **verb** (doing word).

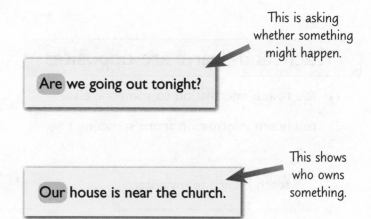

We are paid every Friday.

Are we going out tonight?

This is asking whether something might happen.

2) **'Our'** means 'belonging to us'.

It's our favourite song.

Our house is near the church.

This shows who owns something.

Commonly Confused Words

'Been' and 'being' can sound the same

1) **'Been'** is used after the words **'have'**, **'has'** or **'had'**.

> I have been there before.

> My mum has been too.

> Dad had been before us both.

2) **'Being'** is used after **'am'**, **'are'**, **'were'** or **'was'**.

> I am being careful.

> They are being welcomed.

> We were being friendly.

> Josh was being protective.

'Bought' and 'brought' mean different things

'Brought' is the past tense of **'bring'**. **'Bought'** is the past tense of **'buy'**.

> I brought an umbrella.

This means 'I have an umbrella with me'.

> I bought an umbrella.

This means 'I purchased an umbrella'.

'Teach' and 'learn' are opposites

1) You **teach** information **to** someone else.

2) You **learn** information **from** someone else.

> I teach French to my sister.

> My sister learns French from me.

Practice Questions

1) Circle the correct word to use in each sentence.

a) **There / Their** were **to / too** many people in the park.

b) If we go to **you're / your** house, we can drop off **our / are** shopping bags.

c) He was sacked because he was **been / being** rude **to / too** the customers.

d) Lots **of / off** people **brought / bought** food to the picnic.

e) They have **been / being** painting **your / you're** fence for a fortnight.

f) **Are / Our** you going to the cash point? I need to come **to / too**.

2) Each of these sentences has a mistake. Correct the mistake and rewrite the sentence.

a) She was been too harsh with her criticism.

....

b) They're going to have there wedding at the church.

....

c) I bought some shoes but they were to small.

....

d) Switch the computer of when you're finished.

....

e) My friend learns me how to play guitar.

....

f) He bought a box of chocolates into work.

....

g) Harry smashed you're lamp.

....

h) Their buying a new TV to replace the old one.

....

Writing Test Advice

You will have two tasks to do in the writing test

1) A **word count** may be provided for the tasks. This tells you roughly how much you need to write.

2) **Check** the front of the paper to see **how much time** you have and **how many marks** each task is worth — look for any advice about how best to **divide** your **time**.

Planning is important in the writing test

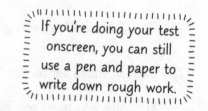

If you're doing your test onscreen, you can still use a pen and paper to write down rough work.

1) Making a **plan** will help you get your ideas in the **right order**.

2) If you're given **bullet points**, make sure you use them in your plan.

> **EXAMPLE:**
>
> You held your friend's birthday party at a local hotel and everyone really enjoyed it. Write a letter thanking the manager for a great time.
>
> You should include:
>
> * why you are writing   It might be helpful to write about the
>   bullet points in the order they are given.
> * the details of the party
>   Your answer should
> * why you had such a great time.   include all these things.

3) You will get marks if your answer has a **clear beginning**, **middle** and **end**.

4) **Don't** spend **too long** on your plan — leave enough time to write your **full answer**.

5) Try to leave some time at the end of the test to **check** your work and **correct any mistakes**.

Write clearly and correctly in the writing test

1) Use **full sentences** and **paragraphs** to make your writing clear.

2) **Spelling, punctuation** and **grammar** are usually worth **about 40%** of the marks, so **check** for mistakes.

3) If you're **copying** a word that's used in a text, make sure you spell it **correctly**.

4) Your **style** and **content** are **important**:

   * **Don't** use **text language** like 'coz' or 'tho', even if you're writing to a friend.

   * Always be **polite**. Even if you are writing to complain, **don't be rude**.

   * If you **make up any details**, be **sensible** and make sure they add something **useful**.

   * Use any **similar experiences** you've had to make your writing more **believable**.

Candidate Surname	Candidate Forename(s)

Date	Candidate Signature

Functional Skills

English Level 1

Writing
Question Booklet

Time allowed: 60 minutes

You **may not** use a dictionary.	

Instructions to candidates

- Use **black or blue ink** to write your answers.
- Write your name and the date in the spaces provided above.
- There are **2 tasks** in this paper.
  Answer **both tasks** in the spaces provided.

Information for candidates

- There are **50 marks** available for this paper.
  - **Task 1** has **25 marks** available.
  - **Task 2** has **25 marks** available.
  - There are marks for spelling, punctuation and grammar in **both** tasks.

Advice to candidates

- Read each task carefully before you start answering it.
- Aim to spend 30 minutes on each task.
- **Plan** each answer before you start writing it.
- Leave some time to **check** your answers at the end.

Total Marks

Writing Practice Paper

Task 1

Remember:

For this Writing Task, you will get marks for:

- clearly and effectively communicating information

- using an appropriate amount of detail

- using an appropriate format and structure (including the use of paragraphs)

- using appropriate language

- using a range of sentence types

- using correct spelling, punctuation and grammar

- making sure your writing flows and reads well as a whole.

Task 1

Information

You are interviewing local residents about plans to build a large shopping centre in the town of Sunnyfield. Here are some of the opinions about the plans:

➢ People will be able to get all their shopping in one place.

➢ It could bring more people, money and jobs to Sunnyfield.

➢ It could put smaller shops out of business.

➢ It might ruin the look of the town.

➢ There is already a shopping centre a 15 minute drive away.

Writing Task

Write an article for your local newspaper discussing the plans to build a large shopping centre in the town.

In your article, you should:

• discuss the advantages of building the shopping centre

• discuss the disadvantages of building the shopping centre

• give your opinion on whether the plans should go ahead and why.

Aim to write around 200 to 250 words.

25 marks

You can use this space to plan your answer:

....

....

....

....

....

....

....

....

Write your article below:

....

....

....

....

....

....

....

....

....

....

....

....

....

....

....

....

....

....

....

....

....

Write your article below:

....

(25 marks)

Task 2

Remember:

For this Writing Task, you will get marks for:

* clearly and effectively communicating information

* using an appropriate amount of detail

* using an appropriate format and structure (including the use of paragraphs)

* using appropriate language

* using a range of sentence types

* using correct spelling, punctuation and grammar

* making sure your writing flows and reads well as a whole.

Task 2

Information

> **Customer Assistant Required — Donelson's Supermarket**
>
> Donelson's is the largest supermarket chain in the UK. We pride ourselves on our fresh, delicious food, as well as our excellent customer service.
>
> We are looking for a customer assistant who will help to keep the Fresh Produce department clean and well-stocked. You will also be expected to help customers. Previous supermarket experience is desirable but not necessary.
>
> To apply, please send a letter to the manager at:
> Donelson's Supermarket Ltd., 48 Hazel Road, Lawrington, LW5 5RR.

Writing Task

Write a letter to the manager of Donelson's Supermarket, applying for a job as a customer assistant.

In your letter, you should:

- say why you want the job

- describe your qualifications, experience and skills

- explain why you are suitable for the job.

25 marks

You can use this space to plan your answer:

....

....

....

....

....

....

....

....

....

Write your letter below:

ADDITIONAL ANSWER SPACE

Make sure you clearly mark which task you are answering on this page.

Answers

Part 1 — Reading

Section One — How Texts Present Ideas

Page 5

Q1 b — A home shopping company

Q2 a — 2002

Q3 You could write any of these:
- London
- Birmingham
- Newport

Q4 a) Explanatory
   b) You could write any of these:
      - It gives you information.
      - It doesn't tell you how to do anything.
      - It's full of facts.

Page 7

Q1 d — From lots of different countries

Q2 c — Over thirty

Q3 You could write any of these:
- ever-popular
- unmissable
- world-famous
- impress
- treat
- not to be missed

Q4 Monday

Q5 a) Persuasive
   b) You could write any of these:
      - It's trying to persuade people to go to the festival.
      - It uses persuasive language.
      - It doesn't use descriptive language.

Page 9

Q1 Email

Q2 You could write any of these:
- 'To' box
- 'Subject' box
- A box for the email text
- A 'send' or 'envelope' button

Q3 Website

Q4 You could write any of these:
- Address bar
- Search box
- Links to other pages or 'home' button
- 'Refresh' button
- 'Forward' and 'Back' arrows

Q5 Advert

Q6 You could write any of these:
- Bullet points
- Coloured writing
- Picture
- Interesting font
- Persuasive writing

Q7 Article

Q8 You could write any of these:
- Headline
- Columns
- Subheadings

Page 11

Q1 b — Alliteration
   c — Direct address to the reader

Q2 Any suitable language technique. For example:
- Exclamation marks
- Rule of three

Q3 a — Exclamation marks
   b — Direct address to the reader

Q4 You could write any of these:
Exclamation marks
- 'Come to Hydro World, the country's biggest water park!'
- 'Book now and kick-start the summer holiday of a lifetime!'
Direct address to the reader
- 'Do you need something to keep the family entertained this summer?'
- 'Come to Hydro World'
- 'What are you waiting for?'

Page 13

Q1 a) Personal
   b) You could write any of these:
      - He uses the words 'I' and 'we'.
      - It sounds like it is talking to the reader.

- It says what Reginald Sprint thinks.

Q2 d — To show that the writer cares

Q3 a) Formal
   b) You could write any of these:
      - It sounds serious.
      - It sounds professional.
      - It isn't chatty.
      - It doesn't use slang.
      - It doesn't use shortened words.

Q4 a — It sounds more business-like

Page 15

Q1 The food was generally very tasty — Opinion
The resort has doubled in size in the last five years — Fact
I thought the cereal tasted unpleasant — Opinion
It has ruined the look of the resort — Opinion

Q2 You could write any of these:
- The coffee was horrible.
- The breakfast was dreadful.

Q3 You could write any of these:
- The resort now has 536 apartments.
- There are six restaurants.
- There are three pools.
- The resort has doubled in size.

Q4 a) Yes
   b) You could write any of these:
      - The author says it's bright, clean and modern.
      - The author describes the apartment using positive words.

Page 19

Q1 d — Give ideas for party games to play

Q2 You could write any of these:
- Coloured writing
- Cartoon boat
- Pictures in the title
- Fun fonts

Q3 You could write any two of these:
- Subheadings
  They break up the text.
- Bullet points
  Make the commands clearer.
- Footnote
  Adds extra information without interrupting the main text.
- Title
  Says what the text is about.
- Different font colours or sizes, bold or underlined text
  They break up the text and make it more interesting.
- The commands are in a box
  This shows they are important.
- Short sections
  This makes it easier to read.
- Cartoon boat
  Shows what the game is about.

Page 21
Q1 b — An engineer teaching an apprentice
Q2 a — There are two people working on another car
   d — It is a bright working environment
Q3 a — 2
   b — 4
   c — 3
Q4 a — You wear protective clothing
   d — You get one-on-one training

Page 23
Q1 The nursery is open from 8:00am – 6:00pm — Text A
The nursery buildings are warm — Text A
The nursery buildings are cold — Text B
The nursery is open on weekends — Both
Q2 You could write any of these:
- The staff are well-trained.
- It's the best nursery in the area.
- Children learn reading and writing skills.
- Children get to do art.

Q3 a) Different
   b) Text A says that there is a "large garden", but in Text B, Eric says that he thought the garden "was really small".

Section Two — Reading for Detail

Page 25
Q1 You could write any of these:
- Search box
- Links to other pages
Q2 c — To tell the reader about Annette's life
Q3 d — She baked cakes for children's birthdays
Q4 Seventeen
Q5 She admires the courage of firefighters.

Page 27
Q1 d — To cover maternity leave
Q2 You could write any suitable replacement. For example:
a) required, essential
b) private, sensitive
Q3 'Discretion' is needed to deal with 'confidential' information.
Q4 You could write any suitable definition. For example:
- communicate, contact
- organisational
- stock, store

Page 29
Q1 c — Overcast with sunny intervals
Q2 Coastal areas
Q3 Tomorrow's weather
Q4 a — It will become sunnier
Q5 Looking further ahead

Page 31
Q1 b — Tickets
Q2 d — Twelve years
Q3 The French Alps
Q4 Contact
Q5 c — Pyrenees

Page 33
Q1 c — To emphasise what she is saying
Q2 a — excited
Q3 Exclamation mark
Q4 d — The support came from one school

Page 35
Q1 b — Sunday
Q2 a — To tell people about Joseph's challenge
Q3 c — 6
Q4 c — Go to the website's home page

Page 37
Q1 c — To help people choose a hotel
Q2 a —To persuade people not to stay there
Q3 a) Sandpiper Hotel
   b) You could write any two of these:
   - It's next to a park.
   - It has a swimming pool.
   - It has water slides.

The Reading Test

Section A (Page 45)
Q1 B — To inform Jackie about the different arguments relating to Sunday hours
Q2 Answers may vary.
For example:
- She is a busy mum
- She works full-time
- She only has free time on a Sunday night
Q3 You could write any of these:
- It would be convenient for people who can't go shopping Monday to Saturday.
- It could create jobs because shops would employ additional staff.
- Shop staff could earn more money by working more hours.

Q4 You could write any of these:
- Sunday should be a day for spending quality time with family.
- Supermarket staff would have to work longer hours.
- You can plan ahead and shop during the week.
- Smaller shops could lose out on business if supermarkets are allowed to stay open for longer.
- You can order shopping online for delivery when its convenient.

Q5 a) Any suitable replacement. For example:
- extra
- more
- further

b) Any suitable replacement. For example:
- simple
- easy
- uncomplicated

Q6 You could write any of these:
- Exclamation marks
- Direct address
- Statistics
- Emotive language

Q7 a) 'leisure time'
b) 'decrease unemployment rates'

Section B (Page 48)

Q8 You get one mark for every two correct answers in this question.
- You can compare prices online — Fact
- Online shopping is risky — Opinion
- A padlock symbol tells you that a website is encrypted — Fact
- You can return any item for any reason — Opinion

Q9 Picture in paragraph 2:
Answers may vary. For example:
- The woman in the photo is receiving something she ordered online.
- The woman in the photo is pleased that her item has arrived.
- Some delivery drivers wear uniforms.

- You may need to be at home to receive a delivery.

Picture in paragraph 3:
Answers may vary. For example:
- The person in the photo has put their card details into an unsecured website.
- The person in the photo has not followed the advice given in the article.
- The person in the photo has failed to shop online safely.
- The person in the photo has been shocked by an expensive delivery charge.

Q10 You could write any of these:
- Headline
- Columns
- Subheadings
- Bullet points / Numbering
- Paragraphs
- Bold font
- Graphics / Pictures

Q11 The website address should start with https://.
There should be a padlock symbol at the top of the screen, next to the address bar.

Q12 Punctuation mark: Exclamation mark
Effect: You could write any of these:
- It makes the sentence seem important
- It makes the sentence seem urgent
- It emphasises the command to the reader

Q13 a) C — To advise the reader about shopping safely online
b) Examples may vary. Some examples include:
- 'you can make sure your online shopping experience is as safe and satisfactory as possible'
- 'Beware of prices that look too good to be true'
- 'make sure you check before buying anything'
- 'always check that:
  - the website address starts with https://'
- 'Remember: If you're not sure about a website, don't use it!'

Q14 B — Statistics

Section C (Page 51)

Q15 Answers may vary.
For example:
Similarities:
- Both texts say that online shopping is convenient.
- Both texts mention that people want to be able to shop when it's convenient for them.
- Both texts say that it's possible to buy things online at any time.

Difference:
- Text A says that delivery charges are cheap. Text B says they can be expensive.
- Text B discusses the risks of online shopping, but Text A does not.

Part 2 — Writing

Section One — Writing Structure and Planning

Page 53

Q1 a) Audience: your landlord
Purpose: to ask him to fix the boiler

b) Audience: your manager
Purpose: to ask for time off

c) Audience: the council
Purpose: to ask them to fix potholes

d) Audience: shop owner or manager
Purpose: to apply for a job

e) Audience: newspaper readers
Purpose: to argue for lower speed limits

Q2 a) Informal
b) Formal
c) Formal
d) Informal
e) Formal

Page 57

Q1
- Start your leaflet with a title or heading.
- State with the purpose of the leaflet. It's about improving customer service.
- Write your points in a list.

- Put the most important point first and the least important point last.
- Make sure all the points are about talking to customers on the phone.
- Divide the points into sections. You could use the bullet points as a rough guide.
- End with a reminder of why it's important to be polite to customers.

Page 59

Q1
- Make sure you include all the information from the plan.
- Write in full sentences.
- Your writing style should be informal because your audience is your sister's friends.
- Start with the important details, then write about everything else.
- Add anything else that you think your sister's friends need to know.

Page 61

Q1   Glastonbury festival is a big music and arts event held in Somerset. Some of the most successful pop artists in history, such as Oasis, U2 and Coldplay, have played there.

The festival began in the 1970s and was organised by locals. When a farmer, called Michael Eavis, took over the organisation of the festival, it began to grow in size.

Now the festival is held every year, although occasionally there is a break which allows the fields to recover. This means that the fields can still be used for farming.

Glastonbury is not just a music festival. It hosts many dance, comedy and theatre acts. There are also sculptures and works of art around the site.

Page 63

Q1 Make sure your report has used some of these layout features:
- A main heading to show what the report is about.
- Subheadings to divide the information into sections. You could use the bullet points provided as a rough guide.
- You could use bullet points or numbers for lists.

Section Two — Choosing the Right Language and Format

Page 65

Q1
- Include your full address on the right-hand side.
- Write the supermarket's full address on the left-hand side.
- Add today's date under your address.
- Use 'Dear Mr Green' to start the letter. Do not use 'Dear Sir / Madam'.
- Use a formal writing style.
- Write in paragraphs. You could have one paragraph for why you want to work at the supermarket, and one paragraph explaining why you're a suitable applicant.
- End with what you want him to do. For example, that you're looking forward to his reply.
- Sign off with 'Yours sincerely', because you know who you're writing to, and your full name.

Page 67

Q1
- Start with 'Dear Karlie'.
- Write in paragraphs. You could use the bullet points as a rough guide for what each paragraph should be about.
- Use an informal writing style because you know her personally.
- End with something like 'See you soon' or 'Best wishes' and your name.

Section Three — Using Grammar

Page 69

Q1 a) applied
   b) wear
   c) left
   d) passed
Q2 a) dogs
   b) your car
   c) the leisure centre
   d) the manager
Q3 Answers may vary. For example: There were some thefts from the staff room last week. Make sure you take care of your belongings. Leave valuables, like mobile phones and wallets, in your locker. If anything goes missing, please let your manager know.

Page 73

Q1 a) Brian carried a briefcase.
   b) You can write any two of these:
      - I will apply for a driving licence.
      - I am going to apply for a driving licence.
   c) My friend lives in Brighton.
   d) We did the washing up.
Q2 a) drive — drove
   b) were — are
   c) cycling — cycles
   d) will go — went

Page 75

Q1 a) The women chat to the receptionist.
   b) Our dogs like swimming.
   c) There is just one problem.
Q2 a) We could have tried harder to arrive on time.
   b) The bank should have told us about the charges.
   c) I might have lost the key to the filing cabinet.

Page 77

Q1 a) or
b) and
c) for
d) so
e) but
f) nor
g) yet

Q2 Answers may vary, for example:
Dear Fran, I would love to come to your wedding, <u>but</u> I can only come to the reception. I can't come to the ceremony <u>because</u> I am working until 6:30 pm. I'll be serving customers <u>while</u> you sign the register! A friend has offered to drive me to the reception <u>after</u> my shift at work ends. There's not usually much traffic near your venue, <u>so</u> I should be there on time.

Section Four — Using Correct Punctuation

Page 79

Q1 a) She used to go to Cumbria every year<u>.</u>
b) <u>T</u>hey only like going on holiday in Britain<u>.</u>
c) <u>P</u>lease tell me what your favourite holiday was<u>.</u>
d) I said that <u>I</u> prefer Wales<u>.</u> <u>I</u>t never rains there<u>.</u>
('I' is always a capital, no matter where it comes in a sentence.)
e) <u>W</u>e always go to Scotland on holiday<u>.</u> <u>I</u>t's really warm in the summer<u>.</u>
f) My favourite holiday was a trip to Malta<u>.</u> <u>I</u>t felt like home except it was much hotter<u>.</u>

Q2 a) Exclamation mark
b) Question mark
c) Full stop
d) Exclamation mark
e) Question mark
f) Full stop
g) Question mark

Page 81

Q1 I want to paint my living room either yellow<u>,</u> cream or ivory.

Q2 a) they<u>'</u>ve
b) can<u>'</u>t
c) you<u>'</u>re
d) I<u>'</u>m

Q3 a) its
b) it's

Q4 She did not want to go to Aminta's party.

Section Five — Using Correct Spelling

Page 83

Q1 a) thief
b) neighbour
(word is spelt correctly)
c) ceiling
d) weird
e) piece
(word is spelt correctly)
f) receipt

Q2 Answers may vary. For example:
Because = <u>B</u>ig <u>E</u>lephants <u>C</u>an <u>A</u>lways <u>U</u>nderstand <u>S</u>mall <u>E</u>lephants.

Page 85

Q1 a) comb<u>s</u>
b) li<u>ves</u>
c) fox<u>es</u>
d) duti<u>es</u>
e) watch<u>es</u>
f) moose (plural is the same)

Q2 a) The caterers need six loa<u>ves</u> for the par<u>ties</u>.
b) The shop sells penkni<u>ves</u> and torch<u>es</u>.
c) Please give the lad<u>ies</u> their room key<u>s</u>.
d) There are a few beach<u>es</u> close to the hotel<u>s</u>.

Page 87

Q1 a) disgraceful
b) happier
(word is spelt correctly)
c) fatter
(word is spelt correctly)
d) regretted
e) betting
f) cleverly

Q2 a) He was <u>taking</u> his brother to a <u>writing</u> class.
b) It's <u>unlucky</u> that he's <u>misplaced</u> the ticket.
c) She <u>disagreed</u> that I'd <u>misspent</u> my youth.

Page 89

Q1 a) <u>A lot</u> of people think fox-hunting is wrong.
b) He <u>may be</u> catching an earlier flight.
c) I <u>surprised</u> my mum with a bunch of flowers.
d) Is Maxine <u>definitely</u> going on maternity leave?
e) Owning a car is <u>unnecessary</u> if you live in a city.
f) The <u>efficiency</u> of her work earned her a promotion.

Page 93

Q1 a) There   too
b) your   our
c) being   to
d) of   brought
e) been   your
f) Are   too

Q2 a) She was <u>being</u> too harsh with her criticism.
b) They're going to have <u>their</u> wedding at the church.
c) I bought some shoes but they were <u>too</u> small.
d) Switch the computer <u>off</u> when you're finished.
e) My friend <u>teaches</u> me how to play guitar.
f) He <u>brought</u> a box of chocolates into work.
g) Harry smashed <u>your</u> lamp.
h) <u>They're</u> buying a new TV to replace the old one.

The Writing Test

Task 1 (Page 97)

There are 15 marks available for how you write your answer.
A top-level answer will:

- Communicate information clearly using a formal and polite style.
- Be long and detailed enough for its audience and purpose.
- Use an appropriate format and structure, including paragraphs.
- Use a range of sentence types accurately.
- Use a range of appropriate vocabulary.
- Make sure everything flows and the writing works as a whole.

There are 10 marks available for the spelling, punctuation and grammar of your answer.
A top-level answer will:

- Use grammar and punctuation correctly and with few errors.
- Spell words, including specialist words, correctly and with few errors.

Your article should include:

- The benefits that the new shopping centre could bring, e.g. 'The new shopping centre will make it easier for Sunnyfield residents to get all their shopping in one place.'
- The disadvantages that the new shopping centre could bring, e.g. 'Large shops could damage smaller local businesses.'
- Whether you think the new shopping centre is a good idea, e.g. 'Despite concerns, the new shopping centre will bring many people to Sunnyfield, and this will bring money to the town.'

You should set your article out correctly:

- Write a title to show what your article is about, e.g. 'Advantages and Disadvantages of the New Sunnyfield Shopping Centre'.
- Use subheadings to separate the different sections of your article.
- Group similar points together.

- Use bullet points or numbered lists to show information more clearly.

Your article should have a clear structure:

- Start with an introduction to explain what the article is about.
- Describe the benefits of the new shopping centre.
- Describe the disadvantages of the new shopping centre.
- Write a conclusion to say what you think the people of Sunnyfield should do based on the benefits and disadvantages, e.g. 'To protect Sunnyfield, the people of the town should start a petition and send it to their MP' or 'Sunnyfield should welcome this new shopping centre and all the benefits it will bring with it'.
- Use paragraphs and full sentences.

Task 2 (Page 102)

There are 15 marks available for how you write your answer.
A top-level answer will:

- Communicate information clearly using a formal and polite style.
- Be long and detailed enough for its audience and purpose.
- Use an appropriate format and structure, including paragraphs.
- Use a range of sentence types accurately.
- Use a range of appropriate vocabulary.
- Make sure everything flows and the writing works as a whole.

There are 10 marks available for the spelling, punctuation and grammar of your answer.
A top-level answer will:

- Use grammar and punctuation correctly and with few errors.
- Spell words, including specialist words, correctly and with few errors.

Your letter should include:

- Why you want to work for Donelson's Supermarket, e.g. 'I enjoy helping customers.'
- What qualifications, experience and skills you have, e.g. 'I have two years of retail experience.'
- Why you are suitable for the job, e.g. 'I am hard-working and previously held a job which involved communicating with customers.'

You should set your letter out correctly:

- Write your address and the date at the top right-hand side of the page.
- Write the supermarket's full address on the left-hand side of the page, underneath your information:

    The Manager,
    Donelson's Supermarket Ltd.,
    48 Hazel Road,
    Lawrington,
    LW5 5RR

- Start with 'Dear Sir / Madam' because you don't know who you're writing to.
- End the letter with 'Yours faithfully'.

Your letter should have a clear structure:

- Start with the purpose of the letter, e.g. 'I am writing to apply...'
- Go on to say why you want the job, what qualifications, experience and skills you have, and why you would be suitable for the job.
- End with what you want them to do, e.g. 'I look forward to hearing from you soon.'
- Use paragraphs and full sentences. Start a new paragraph for each point.

Glossary

A

Advertisement (advert)

A text that persuades the reader to do something, e.g. buy a product or visit an attraction.

Alliteration

The repetition of sounds or letters at the beginning of words that are close together.

Apostrophe

A punctuation mark that shows missing letters in a word or that something belongs to someone.

Article

A text from a newspaper or magazine.

Audience

The person or people who read a text.

B

Bullet points

A way of breaking up information into separate points in a list.

C

Caption

Text that tells you more about a graphic.

Comma

A punctuation mark that is used to separate different items in a list.

D

Descriptive writing

Writing that tells the reader what something is like in detail.

Direct address

Writing that uses 'you' to address the reader directly.

E

Email

An electronic message sent from one computer to another.

Explanatory writing

Writing that tells the reader about something. It usually uses a lot of facts.

F

Font

How letters look when they are typed, e.g. **bold** or *italics*.

Footnote

Extra information at the bottom of a page. Shown by small, raised numbers or symbols within a text.

Formal writing

Writing that sounds serious and professional.

Format

How texts are laid out on a page.

G

Glossary

A part of a text which explains the meaning of difficult words.

Graphic

A picture, diagram or chart.

I

Impersonal writing

Writing that doesn't tell you anything about the writer's personality or opinions.

Informal writing

Writing that sounds chatty and friendly.

Instructive writing

Writing that tells the reader how to do something.

Layout

How a text is presented on the page using different presentational features.

Leaflet

A text that gives the reader information about something.

Letter

A text written to a person, or a group of people, which is sent in the post.

Personal writing

Writing that is written from the writer's point of view. It is full of opinions and emotions. It sounds like it's talking to the reader.

Persuasive writing

Writing that tries to convince the reader to do or feel something.

Prefixes

Letters added to the start of a word which change the word's meaning.

Presentational features

Any part of the text which affects the layout. For example, headings, subheadings, bullet points, paragraphs, graphics or captions.

Purpose

The reason a text is written.

Report

A text that gives the reader information about something that has happened or might happen.

Rule of three

Using three parts of a sentence, e.g. verbs, nouns or adjectives, to create a particular effect.

Shortened word

A word that has been shortened by replacing a letter with an apostrophe, e.g. 'didn't' or 'hasn't'.

Silent letters

Letters in a word which you can't hear when the word is said aloud, for example the 'b' in lamb.

Specialist words

Words specific to particular subjects or topics.

Style

How a text is written, e.g. formally or informally.

Suffixes

Letters added to the end of a word which change the word's meaning.

Tense

Whether a verb is talking about an action in the past or the present.

Text type

The kind of text, e.g. an article, report, letter, email, blog or webpage.

Tone

The way a text sounds to the reader. For example, personal or impersonal.

Webpage

A type of text found on a website.

Index